HAUNTED AMERICA

Ghost Stories and True Tales of Terror

Publications International, Ltd.

Contributing Writers: Jeff Bahr, Linda Godfrey, J. K. Kelley, Suzanne Reisman, Michael Riedlinger, Russell Roberts, Adam Selzer, Sue Sveum, Donald Vaughan, James Willis

Factual Verification: Hollie Deese, Kathryn L. Holcomb, Carl Miller, Christy Nadalin

Cover Illustration: Adrian Chesterman

Interior Illustrations: Dan Grant, iStockphoto, Jupiterimages, Robert Schoolcraft, Shutterstock, Thinkstock, John Zielinski

Louis Weber, CEO
Publications International, Ltd.
7373 North Cicero Avenue
Lincolnwood, Illinois 60712

ISBN-13: 978-1-4508-4377-5
ISBN-10: 1-4508-4377-8

Manufactured in USA.

8 7 6 5 4 3 2 1

Contents

Be Sure to Check Under the Bed!

Being scared can be kind of fun. Isn't it sort of cool to experience a little shiver when you hear or read a creepy story or watch a scary movie? With a host of ghost stories and terrifying tales of the paranormal, *Haunted America* is sure to give you thrills and chills.

These are true tales (or so we're told) of the weird and wicked, the spectral and spirited, the creepy and cryptic. Some are intriguing, some are funny, and some will have you scratching your head in disbelief. But don't say we didn't warn you. The stories in this book may give you goose bumps or make the hairs on the back of your neck stand up. And after reading a tale or two, you may even feel the urge to look under your bed or double-check that the closet door is closed before you go to sleep—you know, *just in case.*

Inside *Haunted America,* you'll find plenty of fascinating and frightening facts as well as horrifying tales of visits from the "Other Side." We've also consulted paranormal experts who share what their job is *really* like and answer some burning questions about ghosts.

Still skeptical? Here's a taste of what we have in store for you:

- In the late 1980s and early 1990s, a woman in California and the paranormal investigators who tried to help her were stalked by the angry spirit of a murdered sailor.

- Restless spirits of slaves who were tortured and maimed by their owner continue to haunt the LaLaurie Mansion in New Orleans. Several apparitions have been spotted there, including the ghost of a naked slave in chains that reportedly attacked a former resident before vanishing into thin air.
- A doll named "Annabelle" was possessed by a demon in the 1970s. The doll changed positions on its own and even attacked a young man. It is now kept in a museum of the occult in Connecticut.
- In the late 1890s, Zona Heaster Shue died under mysterious circumstances. Her husband was arrested for the crime. When the case went to court, Zona's mother told the jury that her daughter's ghost had come to her in a dream to name the husband as the killer. Did the jury believe her?
- A family in Wisconsin was tormented by an evil spirit that invaded their home when they bought a set of used bunk beds. Did getting rid of the bunk beds get rid of the demon? Read on to find out.

See what we mean? *Haunted America* is packed with tales of paranormal phenomena and events with no scientific explanation. So sit back, relax, and get ready for a scary ride.

Everything You Always Wanted to Know About Ghosts but Were Afraid to Ask

When it comes to ghosts, there are believers and nonbelievers. Wherever you stand, you have to admit that the thought of life after death is pretty cool. But how much do you really know about the spirit world? Read on for answers to some of the most common questions about ghosts.

So What *Is* a Ghost, Anyway?

A ghost is simply the spirit or soul of a person who has died but hasn't made it to the "Other Side." In other words, it's caught between this world and the next. Ghosts are made up of energy, and they exist without a physical body. They are often the spirits of people who died suddenly and were not prepared for death. Sometimes ghosts appear to warn or guide family members or to share in happy times.

Why Can Kids See Ghosts More Easily than Adults?

Children are more sensitive to seeing spirits for many reasons. First, they are generally more open-minded and willing to accept things that are new and different. Also, spiritually speaking, children are more closely connected to their heavenly origins than adults. And adults may not want to admit that they saw a ghost for fear of being ridiculed.

Can Ghosts Cross Water?

Some people may disagree, but the short answer is yes. In fact, most experts think that ghosts are actually *attracted* to water. After all, spirits are made up of energy, and nothing conducts energy better than water. That's why a lot of paranormal activity takes place on and near bodies of water.

Can Ghosts Really Float Above the Ground?

Yep. Like we said, ghosts are made up of energy. And experts in the ghost-hunting business believe that the spirit world works a bit like electricity. Ghosts appear to float because when they touch the ground, they are absorbed by the earth. That doesn't mean that all ghosts float through the air. Some seem to be walking without their feet touching the ground.

Can Ghosts Attach Themselves to People?

Definitely. Some spirits remain earthbound because they have unfinished business here. They are usually drawn to specific locations—like places where they lived, worked, or died. They may also be attracted to people who cause them to feel strong emotions—either good or bad. Sometimes, a ghost will even attach itself to a stranger because that person can see or hear it. But that connection usually only lasts until the spirit's earthly issues are resolved and it crosses over to the Other Side. So don't worry—the chances of a ghost stalking you are pretty slim.

How Do Ghosts Move Things or Mess with Electrical Devices?

Ghosts use energy—both their own and borrowed power—to move objects, make noises, play tricks, and get people's attention. Spirits can also gather extra fuel from electronic and battery-powered objects. It takes a lot of energy for spirits to get our attention, so they need to stock up on fuel in order to make their presence known. That's why at haunted places, fully charged batteries sometimes die really quickly and other electronic equipment goes berserk, like the TV turning on by itself at a really high volume or the lights flickering on and off.

Where Is the Best Place to See a Ghost?

Ghosts can be found just about anywhere, but they seem to like hanging out at cemeteries, old houses, battlefields, hospitals, colleges, and restaurants. Happy hunting!

The Cave of the Murderous Witch

There have been ghostly encounters in almost every small town in the world. But Adams, Tennessee, might be the only place where a ghost was held responsible for the death of a human being.

Meet the Bell Family

In 1817, John Bell Sr. was inspecting a field on his farm in northern Tennessee. That's when he came across a strange beast that he described as doglike with a rabbitlike head. When John shot at the creature, it ran into the woods.

A short time later, the Bell family started to experience odd things in their home. It started out as soft knocks, but soon, it sounded like an animal was biting or gnawing on the house. The Bell family searched the building for mice, but they found nothing. Next, they heard what sounded like rocks hitting the house. And then, it sounded like rocks were being thrown from *inside* the house. Once again, the family's searches turned up nothing.

John Bell and his youngest daughter, Betsy, were also attacked by an unseen force. Betsy was frequently pushed, grabbed, and slapped by the invisible intruder.

John Bell asked his neighbors if they had any ideas about what was occurring. The neighbors spent some time in the Bell home and witnessed the unusual activity themselves. They suggested conducting an investigation. John Bell reluctantly agreed, and several friends were invited over.

The Investigations Begin

When the investigation began, thumping sounds were heard throughout the house. Soon the thumps and groans began to sound like someone growling or clearing his or her throat. And then it happened: The creature began to speak. It said that it wanted to stop Betsy Bell from marrying a local boy named Joshua Gardner. It also said that it wanted to kill John Bell.

When asked why it wanted to break up Betsy and Joshua and kill John, the voice remained silent. But one night, the voice said that it was the spirit of Kate Batts, a neighbor who had disliked John Bell because of some unfriendly business dealings between them in the past. Whether or not it was actually the spirit of Kate Batts is unknown, but people began to refer to the entity as "Kate."

Kate liked to have long discussions with those present. She would often quote from the Bible, which was a rather odd thing for an evil spirit to do. She also seemed to know exactly what people were doing at any given time, even if they were miles away.

Soon, word of the "Bell Witch" spread throughout the area, and people came from all over to witness it. One legend states that when General Andrew Jackson and his men passed through the area, the future president decided that he wanted to hear Kate for himself. But the witch caused Jackson's wagons to stop right at the Bell property line and wait more than 30 minutes before she allowed them to continue. When Jackson's party got to the Bell home, the witch cried out that there were two frauds in Jackson's group and that she would expose them. But Jackson and his men left quickly the next morning without finding out who the frauds were. Jackson later declared, "I'd rather fight the entire British Army than deal with the Bell Witch."

The Torment Continues

The activity at the Bell house went on for almost three years. And even though Betsy was under constant attack,

John Bell was the main target of the witch's abuse. From time to time, John would fall deathly ill. Sometimes his tongue swelled so badly that he could barely speak or swallow, and no medications helped. After some time, John would simply recover and seem fine... until the next time that he would be stricken with a mysterious illness. All the while, the witch would laugh and taunt John, claiming that one day, she would kill him.

On December 20, 1820, John Bell was found dead in his bed. Next to his bed, his family found a new medicine bottle that contained a mysterious liquid. John's son stuck his finger in the bottle and then got a cat to lick the substance off. The cat died almost immediately. At that moment, it became clear to everyone that the witch had poisoned John Bell.

When John was laid to rest in the family cemetery, some people reported hearing the Bell Witch laugh out loud at the fact that she had succeeded in her mission to kill him.

Unfinished Business

But Kate's work wasn't done. She continued to focus on breaking up Betsy and Joshua Gardner. Finally, in the spring of 1821, Betsy ended the relationship. After that, the Bell Witch left, but she promised to return in seven years to check up on the family.

According to legend, Kate did return in 1828. At that time, she visited the home of John Bell Jr. She apparently stayed for several weeks and had many casual conversations with John Jr. But she refused to explain why she had killed John Sr. or why she wanted to break up Betsy and Joshua.

Before Kate left again, she promised to return in 107 years. But 1935 came and went without the Bell Witch making an appearance. Or maybe she never really left the area.

Down into the Cave

A large cave is located on the former property of John Bell. Many people believe that the Bell Witch hung out in this cave when she was not actively haunting the Bell family. Others believe that the cave represents some sort of portal or entrance through which she would travel between this world and the next.

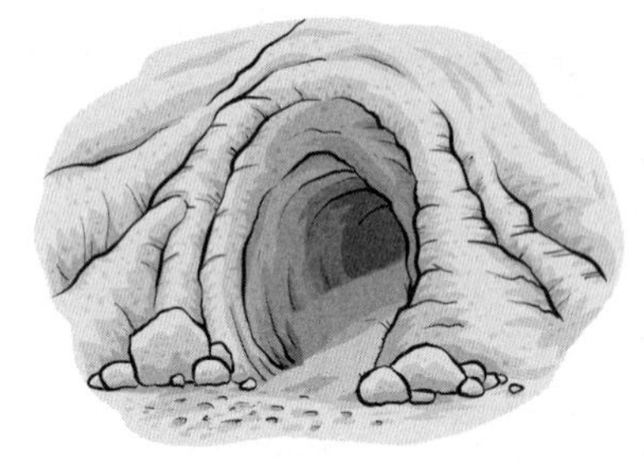

These days, the cave is open for tours. It is still a hot spot for supernatural activity. People have witnessed strange sounds, moving shadows, and eerie mists that appear in photographs. So if you're looking for a chance to encounter a murderous spirit, stop by the Bell Witch Cave...but beware if your last name is Bell.

Gearing Up for Ghosts

Back in the old days, the most common tools brought on ghost hunts were guns and swords. Exactly what those items would do to the already dead is anyone's guess. But if the "ghost" they found turned out to be a guy in a white sheet, the hunt would've had an awfully bad ending.

By the 1930s, ghost hunts involved cameras, tape measures, string, and other household items. Even today, a very credible ghost hunt can be conducted with objects that are found around the house.

In the early 2000s, the popularity of ghost-hunting shows on TV introduced many new gadgets to wannabe paranormal investigators. Some of these can help rule out scientific explanations for weird noises, while others simply pinpoint the best location for seeing a ghost. Here are some of the coolest tools that ghost hunters use today.

Electromagnetic Field (EMF) Detectors

The EMF detector is one of the most popular gizmos in the ghost hunter's toolbox. As you've already learned, a ghost is nothing more than a form of energy. An EMF detector allows investigators to track changes in the electromagnetic energy in a specific area. (Electromagnetic energy is a combination of electrical and magnetic waves that are emitted by objects, even spirits.) If the reading on an EMF detector suddenly jumps, it may be a sign that a ghost is present. But keep in mind that electrical outlets, TV sets, and other appliances also give off electromagnetic energy and can cause EMF detectors to go crazy. You'll want to rule out these things before concluding that a spike in EMF was caused by a ghost.

EMF detectors come in a variety of shapes and sizes. Prices range from about $30 for a simple model that you'll have to leave sitting on the ground to hundreds of dollars for a version that you can carry with you.

Cameras

Use the best camera that you can. A camera-phone is better than nothing, but no skeptic is going to be swayed by a photo taken with a cell phone. Many phones take pictures that have a lot of "noise"—specks and blobs of light that can easily be mistaken for a ghost.

Ghost hunters disagree about which is better: a film camera or a digital model. Digital cameras can be useful for documenting locations, but they do have their flaws. Older and less expensive models tend to pick up a lot of "orbs." (Some believe orbs are balls of spirit energy, but skeptics say they're just dust particles or light bouncing off an object.) Digital cameras also eliminate some of the issues associated with film cameras, like double exposures and overexposures, which can be mistaken for ghostly images. But newer, high-end models are good enough that most investigators think that they're fine to take on ghost hunts.

Audio Gear

Some of the coolest evidence that ghost hunters collect at haunted places are electronic voice phenomena, or EVPs for short. EVPs are audio recordings of voices and sounds that can't be heard with the naked ear. It would seem logical that if you want to record voices from the Other Side, you should get a highly sensitive microphone. But some mics are so sensitive that they pick up voices from outside the investigation area, particularly in big cities. Once, a team of ghost hunters in Chicago recorded the sound of a muffled conversation while they were investigating in the basement of a haunted theater. They were very excited because they thought they'd picked up an otherworldly chat—until they realized that one of the "ghosts" was ordering an Extra Value Meal. The voices were coming from a McDonald's above them at street level!

This is just one case of "mistaken identity" that can result from audio recordings, which are very easy to fake. Some investigators prefer to use tape recorders rather than digital models. But only a very good tape recorder will get higher quality results than a digital model. Either way, some of the most convincing evidence of the paranormal comes from EVPs.

Thermal-Imaging Cameras

Thermal-imaging or heat-sensing cameras have become extremely popular in the ghost-hunting community because the images they project look really cool on television. But they can also be handy for identifying cold spots. (When a certain spot in a room is much colder than the other parts, it's a sign that a ghost may be present.) Thermal-imaging cameras can also help you read tombstone inscriptions that have worn away. But these devices don't seem much more helpful for documenting ghosts than other kinds of cameras, and they're extremely expensive. Even a halfway decent model will cost thousands of dollars. Still, take one of these to a ghost hunt and you'll be the center of attention for sure.

Night-Vision Cameras

Night-vision cameras and glasses pick up near-infrared light that humans can't typically see. They also pick up a different range of usually invisible light than thermal-imaging cameras. Plus, they're much cheaper than full-color thermal cameras and can keep you from falling over things that you can't see in the dark. Using night vision can also eliminate the need for a flash, which some feel should never be used on a ghost hunt.

Motion Detector

Motion detectors are somewhat useful, but if an entity can pass through walls, it can probably also avoid setting off motion sensors. In ghost hunting, motion detectors are often used for security. Set up one in a room where you've left a camera or an audio recorder running so you'll know if anyone sneaks in to tamper with the equipment. You can also lay down some string or sprinkle flour on the floor. If anyone comes into the room, you'll know because your booby trap will be disturbed. It's not foolproof, but it's helpful.

An Internet Connection

Some ghost hunters like to research a haunted location before conducting an investigation. Others like to examine a place without hearing any stories that could cloud their judgment. Either way, questions always come up during a ghost hunt. Doing your homework about the history of a location and its inhabitants can spare you a lot of time and trouble. You may find that you're looking for the ghost of someone who never even existed or someone who is still alive!

Online resources can help you research a location's past. The fact that a place's story is wrong doesn't necessarily mean that it isn't haunted. It's common for an owner to be mistaken about the history of his or her building. But if you find out that a client is lying, (for example, they say, "We've done a ton of research, and we know that Al Capone killed a guy here in 1937," but you find out that Capone was locked up at Alcatraz in 1937 and that the house wasn't built until 1947), that's a major red flag, and you're probably wasting your time there.

Just about any piece of equipment can be used on a ghost hunt. If you can't afford an EMF detector, simply use a radio, a compass, or anything else you have. If it starts acting strangely or the batteries drain much faster than normal, it might be a clue that you're in the presence of a ghost.

These Amusement Parks Offer Thrills and Chills

Many amusement parks have embraced Halloween. They gear up for this "spooktacular" event by playing special music, presenting Halloween shows, and providing a safe place to trick-or-treat. But the spirits that hang out at the theme parks listed below don't limit their appearances to October. These ghosts are the real deal. Check them out . . . if you dare.

Disneyland (Anaheim, California)

Built in 1955, Disneyland (aka "the happiest place on Earth") was the brainchild of Mickey Mouse creator Walt Disney. But some call it the happiest *haunted* place on Earth. According to legend, the Haunted Mansion ride is full of real ghosts. Possible spirits include those of an elderly man who died there of a heart attack and the pilot of a plane that crashed at the site before Disneyland was built. Also said to haunt the place are a teenage boy who fell through the walkway and a man in a tuxedo who lingers where guests get off the ride. A ghostly boy has been seen crying there, perhaps because his mother scattered his ashes in this scary, ghost-inhabited mansion.

Ghosts have also been seen at the Fire Station on Main Street, the Disney Gallery, the Pirates of the Caribbean ride, Space Mountain, Tomorrowland, Tom Sawyer's Island, Splash Mountain, Thunder Mountain, and even on the ever-cheerful "It's a Small World" attraction.

Kings Island (Mason, Ohio)

For a place that's only been around since 1972, Kings Island is home to a lot of ghosts. People have reported seeing a ghostly child walking behind the games and a phantom figure floating near a restaurant at the park's entrance. Nobody knows the origins of these two ghosts. But three other specters that roam the park are more identifiable. The first is thought to be the ghost of a young man who attended a graduation party at the park in 1983. After a night of drinking, he climbed the park's replica of the Eiffel Tower and fell to his death. In 1991, another intoxicated visitor unfastened her seatbelt while she was on the Flight Commander ride. When she stood up to wave to her friends, she too fell to her death. People have also spotted a pair of eyes glowing mysteriously near a fountain.

Lake Compounce Theme Park (Bristol, Connecticut)

When it opened in 1895, the Lake Compounce resort featured a restaurant, a casino, and a ballroom. In 1911, a carousel was added. The facility is still popular today and has been modernized to enhance its appeal. But the site's dark past may have had some lasting effects on it.

Native Americans originally occupied the land where Lake Compounce Theme Park now stands. In the mid-1680s, Chief John Compound sold the land to white settlers. A few days after the sale, the chief mysteriously drowned in the lake. Some thought it was an accident, but others suspected that he was murdered. And others believed that he took his own life. A short time later, John Norton, who had represented the settlers in the sale, met his own demise when he fell off a ladder.

Many years later, when the park was constructed, a workman was decapitated while building a roller coaster. Other workers were killed when they fell from a ride. A young child also drowned in the lake. Over the years, park guests have heard distant music, witnessed objects moving by themselves, and watched spirits gliding around the Starlight Ballroom.

Disney World (Lake Buena Vista, Florida)

Disney World opened in 1971 and is now the largest and most-visited theme park in the world. Like Disneyland in California, a ghost is said to haunt the Pirates of the Caribbean ride. When the crew comes to work each day, they greet the ghost of a former worker who lost his life during the ride's construction. If they forget to do so or decide to skip the greeting, the ride often mysteriously breaks down.

Other Disney World ghosts include a young girl with long blonde hair who has been spotted on Epcot's Spaceship Earth ride and a young boy who hovers nearby. At the Tower of Terror at Disney's Hollywood Studios, employees have seen a ghost that walks around the ride when the park is closed. This shy spirit turns and walks away after being spotted.

Six Flags Great Adventure (Jackson, New Jersey)

Six Flags Great Adventure is one of the largest theme parks in the United States. It's also the home of Kingda Ka, the tallest and fastest steel roller coaster in the world. One couple had a weird experience while they were taking pictures of the giant coaster. The woman saw a young man who was about six feet tall with curly reddish hair. He was wearing a red plaid shirt. Her boyfriend had also seen the young man sitting next to him on a bench. The pair agreed that he was wearing 1980s-style clothing.

After doing some research, the woman discovered the story of Scott Tyler. In 1981, Scott was a 20-year-old park employee who had died while performing a routine test of the Rolling Thunder ride without the safety bar fastened. If the ghost wasn't that of Scott Tyler, there is another group of likely suspects. In 1984, eight teenagers were trapped and killed in the Haunted Castle attraction when it caught fire. So many tragic deaths have occurred at this park that it's no wonder that so many spirits wander the grounds.

Stalked by an Invisible Entity

In November 1988, Jackie Hernandez moved into a small house on 11th Street in San Pedro, California. She was looking to make a fresh start, but her hopefulness quickly turned into what she described as the "nightmare of all nightmares."

As soon as Jackie moved into her new place, she felt a presence in the house. At first, it made her feel safe—like someone was looking out for her. But Jackie soon realized that the presence was not friendly. Shortly after their arrival, Jackie and her young children heard a high-pitched screeching noise in the house. Then, in February 1989, Jackie's unseen houseguests manifested as two different apparitions. One was an old man that Jackie's friend also witnessed. The other was a floating head that Jackie saw in the attic.

Call in the Cavalry

In August 1989, Jackie asked a group of paranormal investigators to check out her house. Researcher Dr. Barry Taff, cameraman Barry Conrad, and photographer Jeff Wheatcraft had no idea how the case would impact their lives. On August 8, the group first visited Jackie's house. They noticed a foul odor in the home, heard noises in the attic, and captured glowing orbs of light in photos. But they were skeptical of Jackie's claim that she'd seen a phantom head in the attic, so Jeff took several photos in the darkened space.

He left the room in terror after an unseen force yanked the camera from his hands. When he gathered up the courage to go back into the attic (this time with a flashlight), he found part of the camera on one side of the room and the lens on the other, inside a box.

Later that same evening, while Jeff and Barry were in the attic, Jeff was violently pushed by an invisible hand. After they returned to the main level of the house, loud banging noises were heard coming from the attic, as if someone (or something) was stomping above them.

When the researchers returned to the house later that month, they saw a liquid oozing from the walls and dripping from the cabinets. They took samples of it to a lab, which concluded that the substance was human blood. Why it was oozing from the walls was anyone's guess.

Get Out and Don't Look Back

On September 4, the poltergeist ramped up its attention-seeking behavior. After watching objects fly through the air and hearing strange moaning and breathing noises, Jackie called the researchers for help.

Jeff and Gary Boehm (Barry Conrad's friend) were inspecting the pitch-black attic. They were just about to leave when Jeff screamed. Gary took a photo hoping that the flash would light up the room so he could see Jeff and help him. Gary's photo captured the spirit's latest attack on Jeff. He was hanging from the rafters with a clothesline wrapped around his neck. The cord was tied with a seaman's knot. Gary was able to rescue Jeff, who was terribly shaken by his encounter with the evil entity that seemed to be out to get him.

After experiencing a lot of other paranormal phenomena that night, Jackie and the researchers left the San Pedro house, never to return.

You Can Run but You Can't Hide

Frightened for the safety of her young children, Jackie moved her family nearly 200 miles away to Weldon, California. But it didn't take long for the poltergeist to find her. The haunting started with strange scratching noises in a backyard shed. Then, a black, shapeless form was spotted in the hallway of the house. And while moving an old television set out of the storage shed, Jackie's neighbors saw the ghostly image of an old man on the screen.

In April 1990, when the researchers heard that the paranormal activity had followed Jackie to her new home, they drove there to continue working on the case. Besides, Jeff Wheatcraft had a personal interest in the matter. He wanted to know why the entity was focusing its physical attacks on him.

That night, Jackie, her friend, and the investigators decided to use a Ouija board to provoke the spirit. During the session, the table that they used shook violently, candles flickered, and the temperature in the room dropped dramatically. But through the Ouija board, the spirit told them that he was a sailor who had been murdered in 1930 when his killer drowned him in San Pedro Bay. He also said that his killer had lived in Jackie's former home in San Pedro. When Jeff asked the spirit why he was being targeted, the entity said that he looked like his killer. Then the evil spirit picked up Jeff and threw him against the wall. Naturally, he was frightened, but he wasn't injured.

Later, Barry Conrad searched old newspaper records and found out that what the spirit said was true. In 1930, sailor Herman Hendrickson was found drowned in San Pedro Bay. Although he'd also suffered a fractured skull, his death was ruled accidental. Perhaps Herman's spirit was trying to tell them that he was really murdered.

Spirit Stalker

In June 1990, Jackie moved back to San Pedro and rented an apartment on Seventh Street. This time, she had a priest bless the place before she moved in. Even so, the glowing orbs of light returned.

Later that year, Barry Conrad's home was also tormented by poltergeist activity. Objects were mysteriously moved to new locations, burners on the gas stove turned on by themselves, and a broom was left standing on top of the stove. Scissors flew across the kitchen and were also found underneath pillows in the bedroom. Jeff Wheatcraft was again pushed by the invisible force, which left red scratch marks on his back.

The haunting subsided after that. But other residents of the house on 11th Street in San Pedro also claimed to experience poltergeist activity. Since then, it is said that no one has lived in the house for more than six months.

Lincoln Still Lingers at the White House

The mansion at 1600 Pennsylvania Avenue may be America's most famous residence. It's also one of the most haunted. Day and night, visitors and staff members have seen the spirits of past presidents, first ladies, and other former occupants. The most famous is Abraham Lincoln, whose spirit is almost as powerful today as it was when he led America through the Civil War.

Two Wartime Leaders Meet

During World War II, the room known as the Queen's Bedroom was called the Rose Room. While visiting the White House, British Prime Minister Winston Churchill strolled into the Rose Room completely naked and smoking a cigar after taking a bath. It was then that he encountered the ghost of Abraham Lincoln standing in front of the fireplace. Churchill quickly said, "Good evening, Mr. President. You seem to have me at a disadvantage."

According to Churchill, Lincoln smiled at him and then vanished. Churchill refused to stay in the Rose Room ever again. But Lincoln wasn't finished surprising guests.

Lincoln Disturbs the Queen

When Queen Wilhelmina of the Netherlands stayed in the Rose Room in 1945, she was hoping to get a good night's sleep. Instead, she was awakened by noisy footsteps in the hall outside her room. She was annoyed, so she waited for the person to return to his or her room. But instead, the individual stopped at her door and knocked loudly several times. When the queen finally opened the door, she found herself face to face with the ghost of Abraham Lincoln. She said that he looked a bit pale but very much alive. He was dressed in traveling clothes, including a stovepipe hat and coat. The queen gasped, and Abe disappeared.

Abraham Lincoln's ghost may be the most solid-looking and "real" spirit at the White House, and hundreds of people have encountered it. Strangely enough, Lincoln seemed to be in touch with the Other Side even before he died. He claimed that he once saw his own apparition. It was an experience that he frequently talked about.

Honest Abe Sees His Own Ghost

On the morning after Lincoln was first elected president, he had a premonition about his death. He saw two reflections of himself in a mirror. One image showed how he usually appeared, fit and healthy. In the other, his face was pale and ghostly. Lincoln and his wife believed that the vision meant that he wouldn't complete his second term in office.

Shortly before his death, Lincoln had a dream about his own funeral. He said that he was in the White House, but it was strangely quiet and filled with mourners. Walking through the halls, he entered the East Room, where he saw a body laid out for a funeral and surrounded by soldiers.

Lincoln said that in his dream, he approached one of the soldiers to find out what had happened. "Who is dead in the White House?" he demanded. "The president," the soldier replied. "He was killed by an assassin!"

A few days later—on that fateful day when he attended Ford's Theatre for the last time—President Lincoln called a meeting of his cabinet members. He told them that they would have important news the following morning. He also explained that he'd had a strange dream . . . one that he'd had twice before. In it, he saw himself alone and adrift in a boat without oars. That was all he said, and the cabinet members left the president's office with a very uneasy feeling. The next day, they received the news that he had been killed.

Lincoln Never Leaves

Hundreds of people have felt Lincoln's presence in the White House, and many have actually seen his ghost. Eleanor Roosevelt's maid saw him sitting on a bed removing his boots. Franklin Roosevelt's personal assistant ran out of the White House after encountering Lincoln's spirit. And Calvin Coolidge's wife saw Abe's face in a window in the Yellow Oval Room.

President Lincoln's ghost has been seen in many places in the White House, but it appears most often in the Lincoln Bedroom. Abe's bed is now in this room. And during his lifetime, it was the room in which he signed the Emancipation Proclamation.

Abe's Other Haunts

After his death, Lincoln's body was returned to his home state of Illinois to share a tomb with his sons Edward and Willie, who had died before him. It took five years for a more elaborate tomb to be completed. During that time, unexplainable things occurred. Visitors reported seeing Lincoln's spirit roaming the area. And after the monument was erected, people heard sobs and footsteps coming from the spot. Cemetery workers had to move

Lincoln's body several times to protect it from grave robbers, and to this day, footsteps and whispers can be heard near his final resting place. Perhaps Abe wonders if his rest will be disturbed yet again.

Considering Lincoln's sensitivity to the supernatural world, it's not surprising that he would haunt Ford's Theatre, where he was fatally shot. Unfortunately, Lincoln's spirit has to share the stage with the ghost of his killer, John Wilkes Booth, who has also been spotted at the theater making his getaway.

Abraham Lincoln played a huge role in U.S. history. His powerful spirit will live on at the White House and in our country forever—literally and figuratively.

RIP RIP RIP RIP

Unsettling Happenings Aboard *UB*-65

You've probably heard of ghost ships or ghosts that inhabit ships, but how about a submarine that takes such spooky folklore beneath the waves? German sub UB-65 *was one such vessel. From ghostly sightings to freakish tragedies that led many to fear for life and limb, the tale of the "Iron Coffin" is an ominous part of military history.*

Das Boot

During World War I, the German U-boat (submarine) was feared above all other war machines. It could sink other vessels from great distances without being detected. But the U-boat had its drawbacks. For example, unlike vessels that floated on the water's surface, U-boats were doomed if underwater explosives were set off near them while they were submerged. But submariners—who are a uniquely brave group—generally accept such perils as part of their job. This makes the fantastic tale of German submarine *UB-65* all the more interesting.

UB-65 seemed cursed from the start. From strange mishaps and tragic accidents to spooky events terrifying enough to scare even the bravest sailors, the incidents associated with the "Iron Coffin" suggest that it was one wicked vessel.

Devil's Playground

Most warships manage to celebrate their launches before any casualties occur on board. Not so with *UB-65*. While still under construction at a shipyard in Hamburg, Germany, a beam broke free of its chain and fell directly on top of a workman. Pinned by the beam's crushing weight for a full hour, the man shrieked in pain. When the beam was finally lifted off of him, the man died.

Later, just prior to the submarine's first launch, a gas leak killed three people in the vessel's engine room. Were such tragedies simply unfortunate coincidences, or was *UB-65* cursed? No one could say with certainty, but many sailors started to believe the sub was cursed.

Chilling Sea Trials

After launching on June 26, 1917, *UB-65* moved into a trial phase at sea. The sub's "shakedown" tests were meant to point out any potential problems that the vessel had before it started active duty. But these tests would prove deadly. As *UB-65* surfaced to perform a hatch inspection, a wicked storm raged outside in the turbulent North Atlantic. *UB-65* claimed another victim when the seaman performing the inspection was swept overboard to his death. This took a heavy toll on the crew's morale, but sadly, even more tragedy was yet to come.

During a test dive, a ballast tank (a compartment that holds water) ruptured and seawater began to fill the engine room. This produced poisonous fumes that greatly sickened all on board. It took 12 long hours before the fumes were finally brought under control. This time, the seamen had survived and had seemingly beaten the curse, but just barely. The next event would turn the tables once again and grant the Grim Reaper his much-pursued bounty.

Kaboom!

If there were any doubts about *UB-65* being cursed, they were quickly erased by an incident that took place when the vessel was being fitted with weapons for its first patrol. As crew members loaded torpedoes into firing tubes, one of the warheads exploded. The blast claimed the life of the second officer, injured many others, and sent shudders through the submarine. Afterward, crew members were given several days off to bury their fallen comrade. It was a solemn period and a much-needed time for healing. Unfortunately, supernatural forces were about to wreak further havoc on the submarine and rattle the men's nerves like never before.

Second Life for the Second Officer

After the crew reboarded for *UB-65*'s first mission, a scream was heard coming from the gangplank. It came from an officer who had witnessed something that his mind couldn't quite grasp. Later, when asked about the incident, the officer swore to the captain that his recently buried comrade had boarded the sub directly in front of him. Soon after, another crewman reported seeing the dead sailor as well. Believing that his crew was suffering from hysteria, the captain pushed on with the mission. But the situation only got worse when the engine room staff reported seeing the deceased officer's apparition standing where he had died. Hoping to prevent a panic, the captain ordered all talk of ghosts to stop.

Everything went well until January 1918—that's when the captain himself became a believer. The turnabout took place while *UB-65* was cruising on the surface. A frightened lookout bolted below deck claiming that he'd seen the second officer's ghost on the deck. Hoping to put an end to spirit-related nonsense, the captain grabbed the lookout and led him back up the ladder. When they reached the deck, the captain's smugness turned into terror. There, just inches before him, stood the ghost of the dead second officer.

Exorcism

With numerous ghost sightings on their hands, the German Navy knew that it had a problem. The sub was temporarily taken off active duty, and a minister was brought on board to perform an exorcism. Afterward, a new crew was assembled and the vessel was put back into service. But it didn't take long for the fright-fest to start all over again. In May 1918, at least three ghost sightings were reported. One sailor was so terrified by the second officer's spirit that he jumped overboard and drowned.

That was the last death aboard *UB-65* until mid-July 1918. It was then that the sub mysteriously disappeared while patrolling in the North Atlantic. No one knows exactly what happened aboard *UB-65*. It is believed that the sub's demise was due to an attack from another vessel, an onboard explosion, or other accidental causes. In 2004, an underwater expedition located *UB-65* near Padstow, England, but researchers still couldn't figure out why the sub was lost.

What is known for sure is that this cursed "Iron Coffin" took 37 souls down with it. The Grim Reaper, determined as always, had received his ill-gotten spoils.

Full Moons Are for Werewolves, but Ghosts Gather at the Crescent

Werewolves must lead boring lives waiting for the next full moon. But the ghosts at the Crescent Hotel in Eureka Springs, Arkansas, keep themselves busy all the time. Some say that the fresh spring water that runs beneath the hotel might attract spirits. Or maybe it's the building's rich history that draws them there.

The Early Years

The Crescent Hotel was built in 1886. It catered to the many visitors who flocked to the healing powers of the hot springs located nearby. The Crescent was billed as the grandest inn west of the Mississippi when it opened, and many folks wanted to stay at this elegant resort.

But perhaps it was *too* grand. The upkeep became unmanageable, and the hotel fell into disrepair. Financial problems forced the resort to close in 1907. A year later, the building reopened as the Crescent College and Conservatory for Young Women. It housed a junior college from 1930 to 1934.

Then, in 1937, Norman Baker bought the property and converted it into a hospital and "health resort." Although he had no medical degree, Baker *considered* himself a doctor. However, the state of Iowa, where he had been living, didn't agree. He was kicked out of the state for practicing without a license. So Baker moved—with his patients in tow—

to Eureka Springs, where he declared that drinking the area's natural spring water would cure cancer. After he was hauled off to jail for fraud, the hospital sat empty for many years before it was opened as a hotel once again.

A Gathering of Ghosts

Hospitals, colleges, and hotels are typically hot spots for ghosts, so it's no surprise that this building is filled with them. Today, at least four spirits are known to haunt the Crescent Hotel. One is the ghost of a young woman who most likely attended college there in the 1920s or '30s. She is thought to have died by jumping from the roof—or perhaps she was pushed. Either way, the trauma of the event was more than enough to keep the poor girl's spirit earthbound.

And if you see a nurse wearing clothes from the 1930s or '40s, don't be alarmed. It's just the ghost of a woman who likely worked there when the hotel was used as a hospital. She's often seen pushing a stretcher down a hall.

More in keeping with the hotel's elegant image, the apparition of a man in a top hat and tails has been seen in the lobby on several occasions. It's believed to be the ghost of Dr. John Freemont Ellis, a frequent visitor to the resort during its glory days in the late 1800s. Near the elevators, visitors often smell smoke from his pipe.

Not Camera Shy

After hearing the bone-chilling tales about the resort, Jason Hawes and Grant Wilson of the television show *Ghost Hunters* visited the Crescent Hotel in 2005. They hit paranormal paydirt when their thermal-imaging camera captured a full-bodied apparition—the jackpot of the ghost-hunting world. The form seemed to be that of a man wearing a hat and nodding his head. Jason and Grant said that in 20 years of paranormal research, they'd only captured a full-bodied apparition on camera a handful of times.

Most Talked About

The most famous ghost at the Crescent Hotel is "Michael," a spirit that haunts Room 218. In 1886, during the building's construction, an Irish stonemason was working on the property when he fell from the roof and landed in what is now Room 218. He died instantly. Guests have heard pounding noises coming from inside the walls and other strange sounds in this room. Some visitors have reported hearing Michael cry out in terror, as if he's reliving his fatal fall.

Ever the prankster, Michael has been known to mess with the room's doors, lights, and television set. Some terrified guests have even witnessed hands that seem to reach out from inside the bathroom mirror. Incidentally, Room 218 is the most requested room at the Crescent Hotel. Go figure.

Room 202 is also popular with ghosts and ghost hunters alike. There, a wispy apparition was photographed in a closet. And numerous ghosts have appeared in and around Room 424. Guests have reported seeing the spirit of a waiter carrying a tray and walking down the hallway past Room 424.

Apparitions have also been observed sitting around a table in the lobby. And a ghostly bearded gentleman wearing Victorian clothing and a top hat has been known to hang out in the lobby and at the bar. He doesn't interact with other guests. He just sits there and stares straight ahead. Bartenders have told stories about glasses and bottles that suddenly rose from the shelves and then crashed back down. Apparently, he thinks that he's not being served quickly enough.

Today, the Crescent Hotel offers the best of both worlds—the modern amenities that guests expect and the romantic atmosphere of yesteryear. And if you happen to see a few spirits lingering, just smile and realize that for some people, things never change.

The Hockey Hall of Fame—Where Legends Live On . . . and On and On

The Hockey Hall of Fame in Toronto was created to showcase all things hockey: the best players, games, and coaches. It's no surprise that legends come alive there—it's a place where stars of the sport live on forever. So you probably wouldn't be surprised to find a ghost hanging around its hallowed halls. But you might be surprised to learn that she has absolutely nothing to do with hockey.

Dorothy Who?

Situated in downtown Toronto, the Hockey Hall of Fame is housed in a beautiful old building that looks like a cathedral, complete with a stained-glass dome. Built in 1885, the structure was home to the Bank of Montreal before it closed in 1982. The Hall moved into the building a decade later.

There have been many theories regarding the building's resident ghost, Dorothy. A lot of people have wondered how she died . . . and why she stayed. Some thought that she was the victim of a bank robbery. Others thought she was involved in a scheme to steal money from the bank and that she took her own life when the crime was uncovered. But most believed she was in a romantic relationship with a married coworker.

In 2009, the *Toronto Star* conducted a thorough investigation of Dorothy and her mysterious demise. With that, the pieces started coming together.

In 1953, 19-year-old Dorothea Mae Elliott was working at the bank as a teller. She was a cheerful brunette, who was popular with both coworkers and customers. She was orphaned at age 9, but Dorothy didn't let her sad childhood get her down. In fact, friends and coworkers described her as "the most popular girl in the bank" and "the life of the party."

But when Dorothy arrived at the bank on March 11, 1953, she appeared upset and her clothing was messy. It would later be discovered that she had been involved in a romantic relationship with the bank's manager—a married man—and when he chose to end the affair, she was heartbroken. At some point, she secretly removed the bank's gun from a drawer and headed to the women's restroom on the second floor. At around 9 A.M., another female employee entered the room and began to scream. Dorothy had shot herself in the head, and no one had even heard the gunshot. She died the next morning at a hospital.

Cold Spots

Over the years, many employees, customers, and other visitors to the building have experienced odd phenomena, all of which have been blamed on Dorothy. Lights turn on and off on their own, and locked doors open by themselves when no one is around. People working in the building late at night have heard mysterious footsteps, and many have reported hearing moans and screams.

One worker who was setting up for an event witnessed a chair spinning around and around until it moved right into his hand. And while performing at an event in the building, harpist Joanna Jordan actually saw Dorothy's ghost near the ceiling on the second floor. When she was invited to play there again, Joanna refused to venture onto that floor alone.

Apparently, Dorothy was so attached to the old bank that her spirit remained in the building even after it was taken over by hockey fans and memorabilia. One young boy visiting the Hall also saw Dorothy's apparition. He screamed after glimpsing a woman with long dark hair gliding back and forth through the walls. Isn't there a penalty for that?

Are There Different Types of Ghosts?

Yes, there are. Paranormal experts believe that there are two main categories of ghosts. The way a ghost behaves can help determine which type you are dealing with.

Residual Hauntings

One type of ghost is known as a residual. The name comes from the term *residue,* or the idea that something was left behind. Simply put, a residual ghost is believed to be nothing more than energy that is left behind when someone dies. Think of a residual ghost as being like an old movie projector that, over time, stores up enough energy that it switches on, plays a short scene, and then shuts off. Residual ghosts always perform the same actions over and over again. They never vary what they do, and they don't interact with the living.

Some residual ghosts are the result of an activity that a person performed frequently while he or she was alive. Other residuals stem from violent, unexpected deaths—which may explain why so many battlefields are supposedly haunted. In both cases, the release of energy leaves an imprint on the area. A violent death typically results in a sudden release of energy. A repeated activity results in smaller, more sustained releases of energy. In both cases, the released energy is stored in a specific location and somehow replays itself from time to time. For example, every night for 50 years, a man would walk from the dining room onto the porch and smoke a pipe after eating his dinner. This routine might cause so much residual energy to linger after the man dies that the action continues to repeat itself. Similarly, a phantom scream that is always heard at the same time of day or night could be the result of a residual spirit reenacting its violent death and its last moments among the living.

Intelligent Ghosts

Unlike residuals, intelligent ghosts *do* interact with the living; they even seem to seek them out. And unlike residuals who repeat the same action in the same place, intelligent ghosts are free to roam wherever they please. So if you sometimes see a particular ghost late at night in the kitchen and at other times in the attic in broad daylight, you are dealing with an intelligent. These are believed to be the spirits of people who, for whatever reason, simply refused to move on after they passed away. In some cases, it's because they want to remain with the people and places they love. Other intelligents seem to have unfinished business here on Earth. And because intelligents seem to be aware of the living, these are the spirits that most often make themselves known to us and to psychic mediums. Unlike residuals, intelligents appear to have the ability to communicate from beyond the grave.

The Black Sheep of the Intelligent Family

Two rather intriguing subcategories of intelligents are demonic entities and poltergeists. Exactly who or what demons are varies depending on your religious beliefs. Whatever your beliefs, demons are very evil entities. They are considered intelligents because they seem to understand that the living are nearby. In other words, demons have been known to interact with humans, which means that they are intelligents. The same would be true for nonhuman ghosts, like those of dogs, cats, and other animals. If spirits acknowledge or interact with the living, they are intelligents.

How to categorize poltergeists is a topic that is hotly debated. Some believe that because humans are the targets of poltergeist activity—like flying plates and glasses—they are intelligents. But others believe that the flying objects are caused by nothing more than violent releases of energy, which would make poltergeists residual. And some even think that poltergeist activity is the result of irregular brain waves emitted by the living, which would make them non-ghostly. So for now, the jury is still out on poltergeists.

Ghosts of Higher Education

Colleges and universities house some of the oldest buildings in America, so it's not surprising that they might harbor ghosts of those who passed through their hallowed halls. Colleges are often home to eternal residents that give new meaning to the term school spirit.

Luther College (Decorah, Iowa)

Gertrude was a high school student who desperately wanted to attend Luther College back in the days before women students were admitted there. She was killed in 1918 when she was hit by a car while riding her bicycle, thus ending her collegiate dreams before they even started. Her ghost is said to make its presence known at a dormitory named Larsen Hall. Students living there have blamed Gertrude for walking the halls at all hours of the night, sounding the fire alarm, and stealing items—especially modern undergarments—and sometimes leaving behind her own old-fashioned clothes.

Eastern Illinois University (Charleston, Illinois)

The resident ghost of Eastern Illinois University's Pemberton Hall was a young woman who was brutally murdered there by a school custodian in 1917. Fortunately for current students, the fourth floor—where the crime took place—has been closed off for years. But maintenance workers still report seeing bloody footprints appear and then disappear on that floor. Residents elsewhere in the dormitory have heard piano music coming from the vacant floor above, where the murdered coed is said to play her spirited song.

Harvard University (Cambridge, Massachusetts)

Harvard's Thayer Hall—which was once used as a textile mill—is now inhabited by ghosts of years past. Spirits dressed in Victorian-era clothing have been seen entering and exiting through doors that no longer exist. They're often seen during the winter months, so maybe they're just trying to keep warm.

Huntingdon College (Montgomery, Alabama)

If you visit Pratt Hall at Huntingdon College in Montgomery, Alabama, you might just encounter the ghost of a young lady named Martha, better known today as the "Red Lady." Martha left her native New York and enrolled at Huntingdon in the early 1900s because her grandmother had attended the school. She was known on campus for her love of red. She decorated her room with red drapes and a red rug, and she often wore red dresses. But Martha was lonely and sad because her classmates teased her, so she killed herself in despair. She now haunts Pratt Hall (which once housed her dorm), where residents occasionally catch a glimpse of a young lady dressed in red. In recent years, students have also reported cold blasts of air surrounding those who are caught picking on their classmates.

Kenyon College (Gambier, Ohio)

Established in 1824, Kenyon is one of Ohio's most haunted colleges. At least three students who committed suicide in different dormitories now haunt them. One rearranges furniture in Manning Hall. One turns off lights, knocks on doors, and flushes toilets in Lewis Hall. Another roams around Norton Hall late at night. And back when Bolton Dance Studio was known as "The Greenhouse" and housed the college pool, swimmers would occasionally hear a voice calling out to them. More recently, dancers have seen wet footprints in the studio, heard splashing sounds, and observed showers in the locker room turn on and off with no human assistance. These strange things are blamed on the "Greenhouse Ghost," which is thought to be the spirit of a male student who died at the pool in a diving accident during the 1940s.

St. Joseph's College (Emmitsburg, Maryland)

In 1810, a Catholic nun named Mother Elizabeth Seton opened St. Joseph's Academy and Free School for Catholic girls. In 1902, the school became St. Joseph's College until it closed in 1973. Mother Seton is buried on campus. Today, her ghost is often seen gliding through the hallways of the school she knew so well. Observers have seen her walking with the ghost of an unidentified doctor who carries a medical bag. Both are apparently still searching for suffering souls to heal.

University of Notre Dame (South Bend, Indiana)

The esteemed halls of Notre Dame are home to several ghosts, including Father Edward Sorin, the university's founder. He is said to wander all over the campus, including in the Main Building and near the famous golden dome. Members of the Potawatomi tribe are thought to haunt Columba Hall, which is located between the two campus lakes—on land where Native Americans once lived and buried their dead. Washington Hall is also rumored to be the home of a few ghosts. Among them is a worker who fell to his death in 1886 and Brother Canute Lardner, who died peacefully while watching a movie there in 1946. And then there's the ghost of George Gipp, Notre Dame's legendary football star. Gipp died of pneumonia and strep throat. Some say he became ill after spending the night on Washington Hall's front steps when he stayed out after curfew and was locked out of the dorm. On his deathbed, he allegedly told coach Knute Rockne that when his players need a pep talk, he should tell them to "win one for the Gipper." Since Gipp's death in 1920, students in Washington Hall have heard unexplained footsteps, doors slamming, and ghostly music.

San Jose State University (San Jose, California)

During World War II, Japanese Americans were forced to live in relocation camps. It was in the old campus gymnasium at San Jose State that these people gathered for processing before they were sent to their new "homes." So it's really no surprise that ghostly voices have been heard talking in a foreign language and crying at the gym. Students there have also heard footsteps and doors closing when no one else is present.

The Haunted Bunk Beds of Horicon

Haunted houses are supposed to sport broken windows, gothic architecture, and looming towers. However, a modest ranch house in Wisconsin shattered that stereotype when it became one of the most famously haunted homes in America.

The small town of Horicon, Wisconsin, is best known for being near a large marsh where thousands of Canada geese stop each year on their migratory route. But in the late 1980s, a small home on Larrabee Street stole the spotlight from the geese when the young family living there claimed that it was sharing the home with a horrific entity.

Nightmare in the Nursery

In June 1987, Deborah and Allen (whose names have been changed to protect their privacy) and their three children began to experience frightening and inexplicable events after purchasing a secondhand set of bunk beds.

The unusual activity began in the room used by Deborah and Allen's son, Kenny. First, a radio would change stations by itself. Then, a babysitter reported that an unoccupied chair rocked back and forth and a suitcase that was stored under the bottom bunk shot out as if someone under the bed had shoved it. Kenny also told his parents that he often saw a glowing old lady with long black hair standing in his doorway.

Fog, Flames, and Fear

As events ramped up during the fall and winter, Allen tried to talk to the spirit that he and Deborah were sure had somehow moved in with them. When he told the unseen presence to leave his children alone, he was shocked to receive a response from a loud voice that told him to "Come here." This was followed by the appearance of a glowing flamelike apparition in the garage. The fiery entity glared at Allen with two large green eyes.

In early January 1988, Allen saw a misty spirit with large green eyes rise out of the floor, and he again heard the loud voice. This time, the voice told Allen that he was dead. Allen and Deborah asked their minister to bless the house, but that didn't help. Rumors about the house being haunted quickly spread around town, and on January 11, the family moved out and threw the bunk beds in a distant landfill.

By January 21, throngs of people who hoped to see some paranormal action had gathered on Larrabee Street. In fact, the Horicon police had to patrol the area because of increased traffic and trespassers. At the same time, the gossip grew wilder. Area newspapers reported that the house had blood dripping from the ceiling, that strange graffiti had materialized on the walls, that the family's snowblower was seen racing around the yard by itself, and that the home's basement had a large hole in the floor that served as a gateway to hell. In short, the gossip was almost scarier than the family's actual experience.

Fame but No Fortune

Milwaukee Sentinel reporter James Nelson tracked down the family at a relative's house. He wrote a series of articles based on exclusive interviews with Allen and Deborah, who agreed to participate on the condition that he change their names. The Associated Press then spread the story far and wide. The *National Enquirer* offered the couple $5,000 for their story, but they declined, even though they had lost about $3,000 by abandoning the house.

Later in 1988, the TV show *Unsolved Mysteries* filmed an episode about the haunted house in Horicon. Actors played the roles of Allen and his son, whose chilling encounters with the evil presence stopped after the family moved and the bunk beds were trashed.

Skeptics claim that the family made up the story. But because the couple shied away from publicity and turned down offers of money—and even suffered considerable financial loss—that seems unlikely. The Horicon chief of police, the family's minister, and the *Sentinel* reporter all stated their belief in Allen and Deborah's story.

We can only hope that the couple buried those bunk beds very deep in that landfill.

This Cemetery Is Number One Among Spirits

In one of the most haunted cities in America, you're bound to find ghosts if you know where to look. And even if you don't, keep in mind that old buildings, new buildings, and cemeteries all attract restless spirits. Among the cemeteries in New Orleans, one is known as the most haunted of them all—St. Louis Cemetery No. 1.

Looking Spooky

When European immigrants first settled in New Orleans, they needed a place to bury their dead. Unfortunately in New Orleans, that isn't as easy as it sounds. The city lies below sea level, so anything buried eventually pops back up to the surface due to the water level. That's why the city is full of above-ground cemeteries where the dead are placed in tombs or vaults. So instead of the tiny tombstones you see in graveyards in other parts of the country, the cemeteries in New Orleans are full of structures that are large enough to hold a coffin (or several). Those cemeteries are known as "cities of the dead."

Near the French Quarter, you'll find St. Louis Cemetery No. 1. Established in 1789, it's a beautiful place that's full of historical significance . . . and ghosts. In fact, many consider it the most haunted cemetery in America.

Just the look of St. Louis Cemetery No. 1 is enough to send shivers down your spine. That's probably why it has been featured in several Hollywood movies, including *Interview with the Vampire* (1994).

New Orleans is known for its many cultures, and the variety of burial traditions on display at St. Louis Cemetery No. 1 showcases this. French, Irish, and Spanish settlers are among the earliest people who were buried there. Today, their marble tombs mix with crumbling rocks. The graveyard's narrow rows and winding paths lead to dead ends and confusion.

It's no wonder that visitors report hearing eerie sounds in this otherworldly place. Is it the wind? Or is it the sound of spirits filling the air with their weeping and moaning?

Ghostly figures and phantom mists hover near the tombs. Some of the spirits are thought to be well-known people; others are anonymous but no less frightening.

Downcast Spirits

One often-seen spirit is "Henry." Poor Henry gave the deed to his tomb to a lady friend to have on hand when he died. Without his knowledge, she sold the plot while he was still alive. So when he died years later, he had to be buried in a potter's field (a cemetery for the poor). To this day, Henry is seen wandering through the cemetery. Perhaps he's searching for a better place to spend his eternal rest. Some say that he has even asked mourners if there would be room for him in their loved one's tomb.

And if you like animals, St. Louis Cemetery No. 1 is a place to see a few ghostly pets that wander among the tombs. All are friendly and are thought to be pets that belonged to a 19th-century groundskeeper. They seem to be looking for their beloved master.

Voodoo Resides Here

The most famous spirit at St. Louis Cemetery No. 1 is that of Marie Laveau, the Voodoo Priestess of New Orleans. She died in 1881, but her spirit still haunts the grounds. Some say that she comes alive each year on June 23 to lead her Voodoo followers. During these periods of resurrection, her spirit is often seen wearing a distinctive red-and-white turban with seven knots. And if you don't happen to spot her ghost, you might just hear her mumbling Voodoo curses. She has also been known to appear as a huge black cat. You'll recognize this specter by its glowing red eyes.

Those brave enough to approach Marie Laveau's tomb will want to follow this ritual: Make three Xs on the tombstone, turn around three times, then knock three times on the stone, and your wish will be granted. And whatever you do, be sure to leave a gift—you definitely don't want to disrespect the Voodoo Priestess!

No Ghostly Groupie for This Celeb

Apparently, ghosts aren't starstruck by celebrities. Actor Charles S. Dutton has been in more than 80 films and TV shows, including *Rudy* (1993), *Roc,* and *House M.D.* But that didn't matter to one ghostly resident of St. Louis Cemetery No. 1. As Charles recounted in an episode of *Celebrity Ghost Stories,* he was in New Orleans directing a movie in 2006, when he and his girlfriend decided to visit the old cemetery to look for the grave of Marie Laveau.

After much searching, they found the tomb and were admiring the many gifts in front of it when they noticed that a nearby grave—which was marked "Duplessy 1850"—had been broken open. The casket was pulled out and its lid was open about five inches. Pure curiosity made them look inside. There, they saw a skeleton with a colorful scarf around its neck. Charles decided to close the coffin and shove it back into the tomb so that it wasn't exposed to the elements. It was getting late by then and his girlfriend begged him to leave, but he kept working.

Suddenly, the couple felt a presence behind them. They turned and saw a raggedly dressed man wearing the same scarf around his neck as the skeleton in the coffin. When the two men made eye contact, Charles felt as if the man was looking straight through his soul. The man eventually turned around and walked away. But when Charles tried to follow him, the man simply turned a corner and vanished. Charles was convinced that he and his girlfriend had just met Mr. Duplessy, the man into whose casket they had peered.

RIP RIP RIP RIP

The Sad Fate of British Airship *R101*

On October 5, 1930, the British airship R101 *crashed during its maiden flight, killing nearly everyone on board. Two days later, a woman with absolutely no knowledge of airships explained the incident in highly technical and freakishly accurate detail. Were the ghosts of the tragedy speaking through her?*

Foretellers or Frauds?

Psychics affect people in different ways. Those who believe in extrasensory perception (ESP) and mental telepathy (mind reading) can find truth in a medium's claims. But skeptics aren't so sure. Psychic researcher Harry Price straddled the fence between the two camps. He hated fakery but had witnessed enough of the supernatural to believe that there was indeed something to it. At his National Laboratory of Psychical Research, Harry worked to separate the real from the fake.

On October 7, 1930, Harry arranged a séance with a promising medium named Eileen J. Garrett. Reporter Ian D. Coster was there to document the event. Harry hoped to contact recently deceased author Sir Arthur Conan Doyle (of *Sherlock Holmes* fame) and publish an account of the proceedings. Like Harry, Arthur Conan Doyle was interested in the paranormal. Making contact with him could bring Harry the evidence that he was searching for about the existence of an afterlife.

Strange Contact

Just two days before Harry and Eileen met, a horrific tragedy occurred. The British airship *R101* (a dirigible or blimp) crashed in France, killing 48 of the 55 people on board. Questions about the event arose quickly. Why had the ship crashed? Who or what was at fault? Were airships unsafe? An investigative team was assembled to answer these queries, but not before Harry Price and Eileen Garrett had their meeting.

At the séance, Eileen fell into a trance and then began to speak. In a deep voice, she identified herself as Flight Lieutenant H. Carmichael Irwin, commander of the *R101*. Her words were as confusing as they were disjointed:

> *"I must do something about it. The . . . bulk of the dirigible was entirely and absolutely too much for her engine's capacity. Engines too heavy. . . . Oil pipe plugged. Flying too low altitude and never could rise. . . . Severe tension on the fabric, which is chafing. . . . Never reached cruising altitude. . . . Almost scraped the roofs of Achy!"*

After the séance, Ian Coster published highlights from the meeting. A short time later, a man named Will Charlton contacted Harry Price. Will Charlton worked at the base where the *R101* was built and was familiar with the airship's construction. He asked Harry for notes from the séance and studied them intently. What he saw amazed him. Eileen Garrett—who had no prior knowledge of or interest in airships—had spoken about one in highly technical terms. More importantly, she seemed to be explaining *why* the *R101* had crashed.

Passing Muster

As details of the crash emerged, Eileen's words proved even more insightful. It was revealed that the airship had passed over the village of Achy so low that it almost scraped a church tower—just like Eileen had mentioned during the séance. She also said that the combination of carbon and hydrogen used was “completely wrong” for the airship. When Will Charlton and other airship officials heard this, they were stunned. Only a handful of project team members had access to this top-secret knowledge. There was absolutely no way that Eileen could've known this information.

Coster's notes contained more than 40 highly technical details related to the airship's final flight. Will Charlton and his coworkers pronounced it an “amazing document.” Before launching an official investigation, they decided to stage another séance. Major Oliver Villiers of the Ministry of Civil Aviation observed Eileen Garrett as she drifted into a trance. This time, she channeled the spirits of others who had perished in the crash. Villiers asked specific questions about the *R101,* and Eileen responded in shocking detail:

Villiers: “What was the trouble? Irwin mentioned the nose.”

Garrett: “Yes. Girder trouble and engine.”

Villiers: “Can you describe exactly where? We have the long struts labeled from A to G.”

Garrett: “The top one is O and then A, B, C, and so on downward. Look at your drawing. It was starboard of 5C. On our second flight, after we had finished, we found the girder had been strained, not cracked, and this caused trouble to the cover…”

Conclusion

When the investigative team's report was released, Eileen Garrett's words matched almost precisely with the findings. After Eileen died in 1970, Archie Jarman—a columnist for the *Psychic News*—revealed that she had asked him to dig deeper into the *R101* case. She wanted to know just how close her description of the event was to reality. After six months of research, Archie concluded that the technical terms expressed so clearly by Eileen Garrett could only have come from the Other Side. In the end, the goal of contacting Sir Arthur Conan Doyle was not achieved, but this fantastic development had advanced psychic studies immensely.

Specters on "The Rock"

Located in the chilly, windswept waters of San Francisco Bay, Alcatraz (aka "The Rock") gained fame as an inescapable prison. Yet one morbid thought comforted the inmates doomed to spend their lives there: Death would finally release them from the prison's forbidding walls. Uh . . . not necessarily.

Sweet Freedom

Today, Alcatraz is one of the most popular tourist attractions in the San Francisco Bay Area. But during its time as a federal prison (1934 to 1963), Alcatraz was a place where hardened criminals and assorted public enemies were sent to serve their time. It was also promoted as escape-proof. Sure, there's the dramatic tale of inmate Frank Morris (played by Clint Eastwood in the 1979 film *Escape from Alcatraz*). On June 11, 1962, Frank managed to flee "The Rock" in a homemade raft along with two other convicts (brothers Clarence and John Anglin). But the success of their escape remains questionable due to the ferocious waters of San Francisco Bay. Therefore, the only surefire ways for a convict to exit Alcatraz were by serving out his sentence or by leaving in a body bag. But even these certainties now seem iffy, since *dead* inmates can still be spotted wandering the prison's halls!

Doing Hard Time

If Alcatraz's wardens were boastful, it was with good reason. Never before had the American prison system operated such an impenetrable fortress. Alcatraz was designed to house the very worst of the worst—mobsters Al Capone and George "Machine Gun" Kelly were once inmates there. And it was built with one idea in mind: Never, *ever* allow the bad guys to escape. The remote island location pretty much guaranteed that prisoners would not try to escape (unless they wanted to be shark bait), as did its high walls, menacing gun turrets, automatic tear-gas canisters, and frequent roll calls. Like other prisons, Alcatraz heaped its share of abuses on the inmates. From the pitch blackness of its dungeon-like solitary confinement (aka "The Hole") to beatings carried out by ruthless guards, Alcatraz has scores of skeletons in its closet. It also seems to have more than its share of ghosts.

The Ghost of Cell 14D

One of The Rock's most frightening ghost stories involves a prisoner who was sent to The Hole during the 1940s. Assigned to Cell 14D, the frightened man screamed throughout his first night in solitary confinement. But he wasn't merely expressing a fear of the dark or fear of being alone in such a scary place. He begged the guards to let him out before the "creature with glowing eyes" killed him. But the man's pleas fell on deaf ears, and the very next morning, he was found strangled to death in his cell. This was utterly baffling because, like all cells in The Hole, 14D was an isolated space with no shared doorways. And it had been locked up tight all night.

The following day, something equally puzzling occurred. During a routine roll call, one too many prisoners was counted. Who was the extra man standing in line? According to shocked guards, it was the inmate who had died in The Hole the previous day. The prisoner was seen only for an instant before he vanished, but it was a moment that none of the guards would soon forget.

Hell's Hallway

Opposite the main visitors' room is a metal door that was once welded tightly shut. It is plainly visible to tourists who visit the site today. In 1976, long after Alcatraz had stopped operating as a prison, a night watchman heard a banging sound coming from the hallway behind the door. When he unlocked the door and shined his flashlight onto the jumble of metal pipes lining the spiderweb-covered passage, the sound suddenly stopped. He found nothing out of place, so he shut the door. But as soon as it closed, the clanging noise returned. Not one to scare easily, the guard opened the door to investigate but again found nothing. So he put the strange incident behind him and continued on his rounds.

Perhaps the guard wasn't aware of the hallway's morbid history. During a bold breakout attempt 30 years before, six prisoners stole some guns and took over a cell house. After two days of trading gunfire with authorities, three of the six men sought safety in the hallway. Despite this move, inmates Joe Cretzer, Bernard Coy, and Marvin Hubbard were ripped to pieces by bullets and grenades. As the shrapnel sprayed against the pipes, it made a distinct clanging sound. Perhaps the night watchman heard the angry spirits of these prisoners reliving their final moments.

Warden with the Willies

James A. Johnston was the first and most famous warden at Alcatraz. He was a no-nonsense sort of guy, so his account of strange happenings at Alcatraz was taken seriously. One day while leading a tour of the facility, the warden and some VIPs heard the unmistakable sound of a person crying. They later recalled that the eerie noise seemed to be coming from inside the walls of The Hole. The sobbing soon stopped, and when it did, an icy cold breeze chilled each witness to the bone.

Another time, during a Christmas party at the warden's home on Alcatraz Island, several guards witnessed a ghostly man appear before them. The apparition wore a gray suit and a brimmed hat, and it sported long sideburns—a style that seemed quite out of place for the time period. As the guards continued to stare at the specter, it turned so frightfully cold in the room that the fire in the wood-burning stove went out. Seconds later, the spirit vanished altogether.

The Musical Mobster

These days, Alcatraz Island is a national park. Not long ago, when a park ranger was going about his duties, he encountered one of Alcatraz's more entertaining ghosts. While standing near the shower room in a cell house, the ranger heard the sound of banjo music. After performing a thorough inspection, he was sure that the shower room was unoccupied, yet the melodious sounds continued.

It should be noted that decades earlier, when Alcatraz's most famous prisoner—gangster Al Capone—was imprisoned on The Rock, he played the banjo in the prison band. In fact, Capone would often stay inside and strum his banjo rather than risk being attacked by other inmates in the prison yard. Invariably, Capone liked to play his instrument where the sound seemed just right—in the shower room.

We'll never know for sure whether this was the broken spirit of Al Capone creating a mournful melody on his phantom banjo or if it was another ghostly inmate, still unable to escape—even after death.

Ghost Hunters Surveys the Rock

In 2010, the paranormal possibilities on The Rock grabbed the attention of television's *Ghost Hunters.* Looking for an especially scary location for their 100th episode, the team lugged their equipment to the island and got down to business. Viewers were treated to the standard battery of tests and measurements—tried-and-true procedures that the seasoned investigators use. But in this episode, they got something more. With their audio recorders, the team picked up an EVP (electronic voice phenomenon) of a voice saying "Harry Brunette 374." A search of prison records revealed that in 1936, bank robber Harry Walter Brunette was convicted of kidnapping a New Jersey State Trooper. He was issued a life sentence for his crime and was shipped off to Alcatraz, where he could commit no more mayhem. Records also showed that Harry Brunette occupied Cell 374. Enough said.

Creepy Haunted Objects

Many people would be frightened to come into contact with a haunted object. The idea is just a little creepy, whether the object in question is a doll, a painting, or a hairbrush. But some people actually search yard sales and surf the Web looking for haunted objects. To those people we say, "Let the buyer beware."

What Is a Haunted Object?

When people experience a paranormal event, they often assume that the building where the incident took place is haunted, but sometimes it's just one item. A haunted object is something that seems to give off a strange energy or vibe. Paranormal occurrences accompany the object itself and begin after the object is acquired. Sometimes, human characteristics—like breathing or tapping sounds—are associated with the item. In other cases, a person may set down a haunted object in one place only to find that it mysteriously moves by itself while he or she is absent from the room, is sleeping, or is away from home. Here's a look at some objects that are reportedly haunted.

An Especially Evil Ouija Board

Many people avoid Ouija boards out of fear that they may connect them with evil entities on the Other Side. This certainly seemed to be the case with the board that Abner Williams loaned to a group of "Goths" in El Paso, Texas. After the board was returned to him, Abner heard scratching noises coming from it, along with a man's voice and the sound of children chanting nursery rhymes. He tried to throw the board away, but it mysteriously reappeared in his house. When a paranormal investigator borrowed the board, a hooded figure appeared from out of nowhere and growled at his son.

A paranormal research team checked out the Ouija board. They found spots of blood on the front of it and more blood on the back. They noticed several cold spots across the board, and photos revealed a strange ectoplasm or foggy mist rising from it. The board was eventually sent to a new owner, who didn't want it cleared of negative energy. We don't know whether or not that person experienced any unusual activity with the board.

Although this is a very haunted Ouija board, it is not an uncommon tale. Many psychics warn that if you ask a spirit to communicate with you through a Ouija board, it's like opening a door between the worlds. You never know what kinds of spirits—good or evil—will use that Ouija board to visit you. So we recommend that you avoid "spirit boards" of any kind altogether.

Haunted Painting

John Marley purchased a painting titled *The Hands Resist Him* at a Los Angeles art show. Many years later, the piece of art was found in a trash bin in an alley. Following strict "finder's keepers" rules, the person who found it took it home.

Unfortunately, it soon became clear why the artwork had been abandoned. The finder's 4-year-old daughter said she saw the children in the painting fighting. So her parents set up a webcam and recorded the painting for several nights. What they saw amazed them—the figures in the painting were moving!

The artist himself had no idea why his painting would be haunted. But he did remember that both the art gallery owner and a Los Angeles art critic died soon after it was sold. Coincidence? Maybe. Either way, the family listed the painting and its bizarre story on eBay and came away $1,025 richer.

Robert the Doll

When Robert Eugene "Gene" Otto was a young boy growing up in Florida in the early 1900s, he had a doll that he called Robert. He took this doll with him everywhere and liked to talk to it. The problem was that the doll talked back—and this was long before the days of Chatty Cathy and other "talking" dolls. It wasn't just the boy's imagination either—other family members also witnessed it.

Neighbors even said they saw the doll move by itself. So when Gene's parents found his bedroom trashed, he said that Robert the doll did it. Did he? Maybe. According to the daughter of the family that bought the Otto's house in 1972, she was terrified when she found the doll in the attic. She said that it wanted to kill her. Her parents had no intention of finding out if that was true, so they gave the doll to a museum in Key West. Visitors to the museum are told to ask permission before they take photos of the famous doll. A tilt of his head means yes, but if you don't get the OK, don't even think about taking a picture, or you'll be cursed.

Nathaniel Hawthorne and the Haunted Chair

You may have seen a creepy old chair or two, but when author Nathaniel Hawthorne encountered one that was actually haunted, he wrote a short story about it called "The Ghost of Dr. Harris."

According to Hawthorne, Dr. Harris sat and read the newspaper in the same chair at the Boston Athenaeum (a library) each morning. After Harris died, his ghost still came to visit. Hawthorne, who was researching at the library, saw it daily. The author said that the spirit had a sad look on its face. The apparition lingered for several seconds, and then vanished. So if you visit the Boston Athenaeum, be careful where you sit—Dr. Harris just might be resting in that "empty" chair.

Annabelle and the Haunted Doll

Raggedy Ann and Andy dolls have been popular for decades. But when a young woman named Donna received a Raggedy Ann doll in the 1970s, she didn't have such a warm and fuzzy experience. The doll would change positions on its own. Once, it was found kneeling—a position that was impossible for Donna and her friend Angie to re-create because the doll's body was so floppy. The girls also found cryptic notes that were written in childlike handwriting. Donna and Angie called a medium, who told them that a young girl named Annabelle had once lived in their apartment building. But after the doll attacked Angie's boyfriend, the girls called in demon experts Ed and Lorraine Warren. The Warrens figured out that "Annabelle" was not the friendly, playful spirit of a young girl—it was a demonic entity. The doll went to live with the Warrens, who knew how to handle its antics. It's now housed in a glass case at the Warren Occult Museum in Connecticut.

Scooby-Doo: The Original Ghost Buster

A favorite cartoon dog has been hunting ghosts for more than 40 years.

The team of Bill Hanna and Joe Barbera created some of the most memorable cartoon characters in history, including the

Flintstones and Tom and Jerry. They also struck creative gold with a crime-fighting pooch named Scooby-Doo.

In 1969, *Scooby-Doo, Where Are You?* debuted as part of the lineup of Saturday morning cartoons. Kids couldn't get enough of the easily spooked Great Dane and his human pals Shaggy, Velma, Fred, and Daphne. Together, the group traveled the country in their van—the Mystery Machine—chasing crooks, hunting ghosts, and solving mysteries.

Bad Guys Revealed

Scooby-Doo, Where Are You? featured a host of ghosts and other scary creatures. The majority of them turned out to be criminals in costumes or masks. More often than not, after catching the bad guy, he would mutter, "...and I would have gotten away with it if it hadn't been for you meddling kids!"

Scooby-Doo and the gang have been on TV almost nonstop since their debut. In 1972, the show was retitled *The New Scooby-Doo Movies,* and it featured the voices of popular entertainers of the day. In one episode, the gang worked as housekeepers in a spooky mansion owned by the Addams Family, who had their own TV show in the mid-1960s.

New Kid on the Block

In 1979, a new character—Scooby's feisty, pint-size nephew Scrappy-Doo—came on board. Since then, two live-action Scooby-Doo movies have been produced (Scooby was computer-generated), and several animated films have been released on DVD. The show remains on TV, with a fan following as strong today as when Scooby and crew went on their very first ghost hunt.

Reaching Out from Beyond the Grave

In 1877, prisoner Alexander Campbell spent long, agonizing days awaiting sentencing in the Carbon County Prison in Pennsylvania. Alexander was a coal miner, and he'd been convicted of murdering a mine superintendent. Although Alexander admitted that he'd been present at the murder scene, he swore repeatedly that he was not the killer.

Despite his pleas of innocence, Alexander Campbell was sentenced to hang. When the day of his hanging arrived, Alexander rubbed his hand on his sooty cell floor and then slapped it on the wall declaring, "I am innocent, and let this be my testimony!" With that, he was dragged from Cell 17 and committed to eternity.

A Condemned Man Leaves His Mark

Today, the Carbon County Prison is not unlike the torture chamber that it was back in Alexander Campbell's time. Although it is now a museum, the jail still reveals the horrors of man's cruelty toward his fellow man. Visitors move through its tiny cells and damp rooms with mouths open wide in shock and disbelief. When they reach Cell 17, many guests feel cold chills rise up their spines as they notice that Alexander Campbell's filthy handprint is still there!

"There's no logical explanation for it," says James Starrs, a forensic scientist from George Washington University who investigated the mark. Starrs is not the first person to express disbelief at the handprint's permanence. In 1930, a local sheriff tried to rid the jail of its ominous mark by tearing down the wall it was on and replacing it with a new one. But the next day, the handprint reappeared on the newly constructed wall. Many years later, Sheriff Charles Neast took his best shot at the handprint—this time with green paint. Despite his efforts, the mark inexplicably returned.

Was Alexander Campbell truly innocent, as his ghostly handprint seems to suggest? No one can say with certainty. Is the handprint inside Cell 17 the creepy sort of thing that legends are made of? You can bet your life on it!

"A ghost is someone who hasn't made it—in other words, who died, and they don't know they're dead. So they keep walking around and thinking that you're inhabiting their—let's say, their domain. So they're aggravated with you."

—Psychic Sylvia Browne

FRIGHTENING FACTS

- *The Los Angeles home of actress Joan Crawford was allegedly so haunted that "Mommie Dearest" summoned a minister to exorcise the ghosts. Several subsequent owners did the same. The unwanted presence may have finally taken the hint because by 2000, it seemed to have packed its bags and moved out.*
- *John Lennon lived at The Dakota, an apartment complex across from Central Park in New York City. On December 8, 1980, he was gunned down near the building's entrance. Lennon's friendly spirit still roams the sidewalk in front of the apartment building.*
- *Since World War I, a pair of female ghosts has been spotted skating at Central Park's Wollman Ice Rink. Both of these spirits wear bulky Victorian-era dresses. They seem to be practicing their figure eights.*
- *At the Altru Hospital in Grand Forks, North Dakota, an elevator runs on its own and randomly stops on floors. The hospital's security cameras have also recorded ghostly presences in the facility's former mental ward.*
- *Fire Station No. 2 in Greenwich Village has a phantom fireman. He's a middle-aged man with gray hair and a large mustache. He wears old-school firefighting gear and roams around the station. Legend has it that he hanged himself after learning that his wife had been unfaithful.*

The Black Angel of Death

Does some evil entity or sinister spirit possess this grave marker?

The statue known as the "Black Angel of Death" is unlike other angel statues at Oakland Cemetery in Iowa City, Iowa. For starters, at eight and a half feet tall (not including the pedestal), it towers high above the others. The eyes of the other angel statues gaze up toward heaven, and their wings are folded on their backs, which signals hope. But with its wings spread wide and pointing toward the ground, the Black Angel stares down upon the grave of Eddie Dolezal, who died in 1891 at age 18. The other angels are made of white marble. But the Black Angel was sculpted out of bronze, which turned black over the years due to oxidation (or, as some say, the sins of Eddie's mother, who had the statue built in 1912). The Black Angel is different from the other angels in another important way: According to legend, it likes to take new victims.

The Black Angel doesn't like to be touched inappropriately or witness public displays of affection. Locals say that girls should not be kissed near the statue. If they do, they will die within six months. Anyone who touches the statue on Halloween night has only seven more years to live. Worse, giving the Angel a kiss can stop a person's heart on the spot.

The Black Angel is said to take its greatest revenge on those who bring harm to it. Legend says that four boys died in a car crash not long after desecrating the Black Angel. Another story tells of a young man who removed the thumb of the Angel. Soon after, his body was found hundreds of miles away in the Chicago River. He'd been strangled and a single thumbprint was found on his neck. Not long after, a blackened bronze thumb was reportedly found at the base of the statue.

Whether or not the Black Angel has actually killed anyone is anyone's guess. But photos do often reveal strange lights around it. One couple found that every one of their pictures featured a red light where the angel's heart would be. Other snapshots have included orbs, which signify the presence of spirits. For whatever reason, the Black Angel does not rest in peace. Anyone in its presence should beware of its powers.

RIP RIP RIP RIP

Samuel Clemens's Psychic Dream

One night in the late 1850s, Samuel Clemens—better known as Mark Twain—woke up clutching the sheets on his bed. His palms were sweaty and his heart was pounding. It had been so real, he thought... so vivid. Was it really just a dream, or did it actually happen?

Before he was a world-renowned author and humorist known as Mark Twain, Samuel Clemens worked as an apprentice riverboat pilot on the *Pennsylvania.* His younger brother Henry also worked on the vessel as a "mud clerk"—a hard and dreary job that was barely one step above being a servant. But Henry stuck with it, perhaps tempted by the possibility of a promotion to a superior position on the steamboat.

While the ship was docked in St. Louis, Samuel stayed with his sister and brother-in-law, who lived in town. Henry often dropped by to visit before returning to his shipboard duties. During a visit in May 1858, Henry was unusually quiet as he prepared to return to the *Pennsylvania.* It was not like him to be so somber.

Did That Really Just Happen?

That night, Samuel saw images in a dream that was frighteningly realistic. He saw Henry lying in a coffin that was balanced on two chairs in the living room of their sister's house. Henry was wearing a suit of Samuel's, and in his hands—which were folded on his chest—he held a bouquet of white roses with one red rose in the middle.

When Samuel awoke, he didn't know whether he had just had a dream or if he was recalling actual events. Was his brother dead? He decided that he had to find out, so he jumped out of bed and ran into the living room where he had seen the coffin during his dream. To his relief, the room was empty.

Later that day, as he drove the *Pennsylvania* down the Mississippi River to New Orleans, Samuel couldn't get the dream out of his mind. Unfortunately, on the trip downriver, Samuel got into an argument with the owner of the steamer and was fired. Henry remained on board.

A Nightmare Becomes Reality

Several days later, the *Pennsylvania* left on its return trip to St. Louis. As it approached Memphis, the boat's boilers exploded with a deafening roar. Dozens of people on board were killed and wounded.

Samuel heard about the horrible accident and quickly made his way to Memphis. He searched high and low for Henry until he found him on a mattress in a warehouse that had been turned into a hospital to treat the accident victims. Henry had inhaled red-hot steam and was not expected to live. But somehow he fought back, and his condition slowly improved.

One night, the agonizing screams of those in the makeshift hospital were getting the best of Henry, so a doctor ordered a small dose of medicine to help him sleep. But the person who administered the drug gave Henry too much. It caused him to overdose, and he died before morning broke.

Henry's body was dressed in one of Samuel's suits, placed in a coffin, and displayed in a viewing room at the makeshift hospital. As Samuel was mourning near his brother's casket, a woman placed a bouquet of white roses with one red rose in the center in his dead brother's hands. Samuel was stunned. His chilling dream—or rather nightmare—had come true.

Henry's coffin was sent to his sister's house in St. Louis. Samuel arrived just before the casket was placed in the living room, where two chairs sat spaced apart waiting to receive it. It was the final detail of Samuel's psychic dream come true.

Samuel Clemens was so deeply affected by his prophetic dream that foreshadowed his brother's death that 24 years later, he joined the Society for Psychical Research, a British group of supporters of paranormal studies.

West Point's Spirited Residents

The United States Military Academy at West Point has an impressive history. Since 1802, it has educated young men (and women, beginning in 1976) preparing to serve their country as officers in the U.S. Army. Prior to that time, West Point was a military fort. With that much history, it's no surprise that these hallowed halls are home to a ghost or two.

Keeping in line with the traditions of the academy, cadets and visitors have reported seeing soldiers from different eras in full-dress uniforms. And in the 1920s, a spirit inhabiting a house on Professor's Row had to be exorcised. It is unknown whether this was an evil ghost or a demonic force. Whatever it was, it frightened two servant girls so terribly that they ran out of the house screaming in the middle of the night.

A cranky Irish cook named Molly is thought to haunt the superintendent's mansion, where she once worked. "Miss Molly"—as she was called when she lived there in the early 19th century—was the maid of Brigadier General Sylvanus Thayer. A hard worker even in death, Molly is often seen kneading bread in the mansion's kitchen.

The Pickpocket Poltergeist

In October 1972, demonologists Ed and Lorraine Warren were invited to give a lecture at West Point. While they were there, they were asked to investigate some paranormal activity that had been going on at the superintendent's house. It seems that, among other things, personal items and wallets of guests had come up missing...only to be found later, neatly arranged on the dresser in the master bedroom.

Lorraine was able to communicate with the "Pickpocket Poltergeist," who said his name was Greer. In the early 1800s, Greer had been wrongly accused of murder. Even though he was later pardoned, he was full of sorrow and was unable to move on. Lorraine urged him to cross over to the Other Side.

Room 4714

But it is Room 4714 in the 47th Division Barracks that has caused the most supernatural speculation. Paranormal activity was first reported there shortly after the Warrens' visit, when students Art Victor and James O'Connor shared the room. One day, when James went to take a shower, he noticed that his bathrobe was swinging back and forth—but nothing was blowing it. Then suddenly, the temperature in the room dropped several degrees.

A couple of days later, James saw the ghost of a soldier wearing a uniform and carrying a musket. The following evening, both boys felt an extreme drop in temperature and then saw a man's upper body float through the room. It hovered between the floor and the ceiling for a few minutes, then disappeared.

One night shortly thereafter, two fellow cadets—Keith Bakken and Terry Meehan—volunteered to spend the night in Room 4714. During the night, Terry awoke and caught a glimpse of a ghostly figure near the ceiling. By the time Keith woke up, the apparition was gone, but both boys experienced an extreme drop in temperature. After the campus newspaper published an article about the strange activity, several other cadets offered to sleep in the room. A device was used to scientifically measure any temperature changes. The coldest temperature was always found right next to James O'Connor. Oddly, one night when other cadets were in Room 4714 waiting for the ghost, James saw the specter in *another* room while the boys in his room saw nothing. It seemed as if the ghost was seeking out James.

Although a significant number of cadets saw the apparition and felt the drastic temperature change in Room 4714, the identity of this spirit remains unknown. The 47th Division barracks are located near the site of a disastrous house fire that killed an officer. The building is also near a graveyard where some Revolutionary War–era soldiers are buried. Could the ghost be one of these military men attempting to bond with the new breed of cadet? If so, the spirit eventually gave up—it hasn't been seen or felt since the 1970s.

The Happiest Haunted Place on Earth?

According to the folks at Disneyland, the Haunted Mansion is home to 999 ghosts... and there's room for one more. But some people believe that the 1,000th ghost is already there—and that it's no special effect! In fact, many spirits are said to linger at the Magic Kingdom long after the last guest has left for the day.

The Haunted Mansion

"Timmy" is the most well-known "real" ghost at the Haunted Mansion. Timmy was a young boy who loved the Haunted Mansion ride very much. In fact, he loved it so much that after he died unexpectedly, his mother asked the park for permission to scatter his ashes throughout the attraction. When the park refused, she was outraged.

As the story goes, Timmy's mother took matters into her own hands. She boarded the ride with her son's ashes in hand and waited until she came to the "Séance Room." There, a harp, a tambourine, and other instruments float in mid-air while Madame Leota—the face in the crystal ball—calls the spirits to come forth and join the party. According to legend, Timmy's mother scattered her son's ashes as her "Doom Buggy" moved through the room. Ever since then, some guests have seen the ghost of young Timmy crying in the area where people exit the ride.

Could the story be true? No one has ever been able to verify Timmy's actual identity. But the park is known to purposely keep the Mansion dusty, so it's certainly possible that human ashes could have been scattered along the dark ride's journey.

During slow periods when they had the ride pretty much to themselves, some guests have reported hearing loud knocks on the backs of their Doom Buggies, even though no one was in the car behind them and no cast members were nearby. Some claim that Buggy No. 55 is the haunted buggy. No one is certain who is haunting it (perhaps it's Timmy), but having a chance to ride in it is a special treat for ghost hunters.

The Sad Tale of Disco Debbie

Another ghost that is seen at the park is "Disco Debbie." During the summer of 1979, Debbie's job was to liven up the crowd in line for Space Mountain—an indoor roller coaster—and encourage guests to dance on the "Space Stage" outside the attraction. After work one day, Debbie was found dead of a brain hemorrhage backstage at Space Mountain. She's since been seen several times, often as a pale green apparition that's visible through the ride's windows.

REAL Skeletons!

Other dead bodies have been in the park known as "The Happiest Place on Earth," and people lined up to see them. Believe it or not, when the Pirates of the Caribbean ride first opened in the late 1960s, realistic-looking skeletons had not yet been created. Their solution? Use real ones! Laugh if you will, but the tale is reportedly true—every skeleton on the ride was real when it first opened, and the skull and crossbones above the captain's bed still are! The story is hard to believe and the company doesn't like to talk about it, but Disney insiders insist that it's true.

And as for the rumor that Walt Disney's frozen body lies in a secret chamber under the Pirates of the Caribbean ride? Well, that's a whole other story!

"Haunting is information received by the witness who has the experience. Hauntings actually show that we are all psychic receivers (clairvoyant) to some degree."

—Loyd Auerbach, famous paranormal researcher

Can Ghosts Hurt People?

One of the most frequent questions that ghost hunters are asked is: "Can ghosts hurt people?" We can answer it by observing stories about ghosts.

To answer this question, we have to consider the different kinds of ghosts. Some are no more than shadows or voices. Others are just blips of energy that cause the needle on an EMF detector to twitch. Then there are the translucent apparitions that float down hallways and the forms that are so lifelike that you'd never know that they're ghosts if they didn't vanish before your very eyes. The type of spirits known as "intelligents" are thought to be able to communicate with the living. Others, which are known as "residuals," are thought to be far more common and are simply forms of energy replaying scenes from their lives.

Each type of ghost has different abilities. Some are capable of throwing objects across a room, or pressing down on a person's chest while he or she is in bed, or, in rare cases, even possessing people. So if some entities can throw things, it's fair to assume that they can throw things *at* the living.

However, the good news is that if ghosts can hurt people, they very rarely do. Some cases, like that of the Bell Witch (see page 10), suggest that ghosts have even killed people. But such cases are so rare that we're still talking about the Bell Witch haunting nearly two centuries after it happened.

But there's also one really scary thing to consider: Ghosts don't actually have to exist in order to hurt people. A person can be shocked into falling down stairs or even into having a heart attack merely by *thinking* that he or she has seen a ghost! And being in an allegedly haunted space can certainly play tricks on your mind. It's never safe to let your imagination run wild when you're tromping around a creepy, dark place.

So don't be too concerned about being whisked away to the Other Side by a ghost. And if you do encounter dishes flying across the room, duck! Chances are, it won't fly directly *at* you. But you can still get hurt if you don't keep your wits about you.

RIP RIP RIP RIP

A True Tale of Possession

Spiritual possession occurs when a person's body is taken over by the spirit of another. Real cases of it are very rare and are easy to fake. But one of the most widely publicized cases happened in Watseka, Illinois, in the late 1870s. At that time, the spirit of Mary Roff, a girl who had died in 1865, inhabited the body of 13-year-old Lurancy Vennum. This astounding case is known as the "Watseka Wonder."

A Troubled Life

Mary Roff was just 18 years old when she died in an insane asylum. For most of her life, she had been troubled by seizures and strange voices in her head. Doctors thought that Mary was mentally ill. But others—including her own family—came to believe that her problems were supernatural in origin.

Lurancy Vennum was born on April 16, 1864. She was barely a year old when Mary Roff died. Lurancy moved with her family to Watseka a few years after Mary's death, and they knew nothing about Mary or her family.

In July 1877, about 12 years after Mary had passed away, Lurancy started to display symptoms similar to Mary's. Her speech became garbled, and she often spoke in a strange language. She sometimes had seizures, fell into trances, assumed different personalities, and claimed to see spirits. It's no surprise that all of this terrified her.

The residents of Watseka didn't know what to make of Lurancy. Many thought that she should be sent to an insane asylum, just like Mary had. But Mary's parents believed that Lurancy was possessed by the spirits of the dead—just like their daughter had been. With the permission of Lurancy's parents, Asa Roff (Mary's father) met with the young girl in late 1877. During their visit, a friendly spirit spoke to Lurancy and asked to take control of her body to protect her from evil forces. That spirit identified itself as Mary Roff.

Sent to Heaven

After Mary took possession of Lurancy's body, she explained that Lurancy was ill and needed to return to heaven to be cured. Mary said that her spirit would stay in Lurancy's body until sometime in May.

Over the next few months, it was clear that Mary's spirit was in control of Lurancy's body. Lurancy looked the same, but she knew nothing about the Vennum family or her life with them. Instead, she knew things about the Roffs that she couldn't possibly have known, and she acted as though they were her family.

In February 1878, Lurancy asked to go live with the Roffs. The Vennums were hesitant, but they consented. On the way to the Roff home, as they went by the house where they'd lived when Mary was alive, Lurancy wanted to know why they weren't stopping there. The Roffs explained that they'd moved to a new home a few years after Mary had died.

Lurancy spent several months living in the Roff home, where she identified objects and people that she could not have known about. On one occasion, Lurancy sat down at the Roff's family piano and began to play, singing the same songs Mary had sung as a child.

Once word spread of Lurancy's spiritual possession, interested people started to visit. During these visits, Lurancy often talked about events that had taken place long before she was even born.

During one encounter with a Mrs. Sherman, Lurancy/Mary was asked about the people she had met in heaven. Lurancy started naming some of Mrs. Sherman's deceased relatives and neighbors. Again, this was information that Lurancy could not possibly have known.

Going Home

After several months, on May 21, 1878, Mary's spirit finally left Lurancy's body. After that, Lurancy stopped having seizures and the other problems that had previously troubled her went away. She did not remember being possessed by Mary, and she came away from it a healthy young lady. She went on to marry and have 13 children.

But Mary didn't abandon Lurancy completely. According to some sources, Lurancy kept in touch with the Roff family. She felt a strange closeness to them, even though she had no idea why. She would visit with them once a year and allow Mary's spirit to possess her briefly, just like it did in the late 1870s.

The story of the Watseka Wonder still stands as one of the most authentic cases of spirit possession in history. Despite numerous investigations, there is still no clear scientific explanation for it.

The Tortured Souls of the LaLaurie Mansion

In the early 1800s, Marie Delphine LaLaurie was the crème de la crème of the high society of New Orleans. Rich, pretty, and intelligent, she put nearly everyone she met under her spell. But Marie had a dark and diabolical secret. She delighted in torturing her slaves in horrendous and despicable ways. Later, the spirits of those who died at Marie LaLaurie's hand would come back to haunt the socialite's stately home.

Social Butterflies

Marie was born in Louisiana around 1775. She was widowed twice and had five children before marrying Dr. Leonard Louis LaLaurie in 1825. In the early 1830s, Marie and her husband moved into the stunning three-story mansion at 1140 Royal Street in New Orleans. It was one of the finest houses in the city. The home also reflected their social status because the family was noted for its wealth and prominence in the community.

As visible members of New Orleans society, the LaLauries often hosted grand parties that were attended by the city's most influential citizens. Like many wealthy people of the time, the LaLauries owned several slaves who cooked, cleaned, and maintained the property. Many guests remembered the finely dressed servants who took care of their every need. But other LaLaurie slaves—sometimes glimpsed in passing—were surprisingly thin and hollow-chested. Rumors began to circulate that Marie LaLaurie was far from kind to her servants.

One neighbor claimed that he watched in horror as Marie chased a terrified female slave with a whip. The girl eventually made it to the roof of the mansion, where she chose to jump to her death rather than face her enraged owner's maniacal abuse. What happened to the girl's body remains a mystery. Some accounts say that it was buried on the property, while others report that it was dumped in an abandoned well.

A Fire Reveals All

The true extent of Marie LaLaurie's revolting cruelty was finally revealed in April 1834, when a fire broke out in the mansion. As the story goes, the blaze was set by a cook who simply couldn't handle any more of Marie LaLaurie's torture.

As the fire swept through the house and smoke filled the rooms, a crowd of onlookers gathered outside. Soon, the volunteer fire department arrived with buckets of water and bystanders offered their assistance. Marie LaLaurie remained calm as she directed the volunteers to save expensive paintings and smaller pieces of furniture. But when neighbors tried to enter the slave quarters to make sure that everyone got out safely, Marie LaLaurie refused to give them the key. Enraged, they broke down the door and were horrified to find several slaves tortured and mutilated. Many of the victims said that they'd been held captive for months.

The atrocities committed against the slaves in the LaLaurie home were extremely repulsive. Some were found chained to the walls, and others were suspended by their necks with their limbs stretched and torn. One female slave was wearing a spiked iron collar that forced her head into an upright position. Some slaves were nearly starved to death, beaten with whips, and bound in painful positions.

Cruel experiments had been performed on some victims. Eyes were poked out, mouths were sewn shut, limbs were removed, and skulls were left open while they were still alive. The men who found the slaves were overwhelmed by the stench of death and decaying flesh, which filled the confined chamber. A local newspaper reported that the bodies of tortured slaves were found buried around the grounds of the mansion.

When word of Marie LaLaurie's vicious and grotesque crimes got out, an angry mob surrounded the mansion. They broke furniture, shattered windows, and stole fine china and expensive food. They destroyed everything that they could find until only the walls remained. But by then, the LaLauries had already fled to France, never to be seen in New Orleans again.

Ghosts Take Up Residence

After the authorities restored order at the LaLaurie Mansion, the property was closed and boarded up. It sat completely empty for years…or so it seemed.

The spirits of the dead quickly claimed the house. People passing by often heard agonizing cries coming from the abandoned structure. Several people said that they saw apparitions of the murdered slaves walking on the home's balconies, peering out of windows, and roaming through the property's overgrown gardens. According to legend, those who entered the building were never seen again.

The LaLaurie Mansion was purchased in 1837. But the buyer put it back on the market after only three months, claiming to have been driven out by weird noises and anguished cries in the night.

Hauntings Continue

In the years that followed, the LaLaurie Mansion was converted into a school for girls, abandoned again, and then converted into inexpensive apartments for immigrant workers. Time and time again, the restless spirits of the tortured slaves made their presence known, much to the horror of the people who lived there. Once, a terrified tenant claimed that the spirit of a naked slave in chains attacked him and then vanished as quickly as it had appeared. Even cheap rent was not enough to convince tenants to stay for very long, and soon the house was vacant again.

The LaLaurie Mansion still stands today. Over the years, it has changed hands several times. It has served as a saloon, a furniture store, a shelter for poor and homeless men, and an apartment building. In April 2007, actor Nicolas Cage purchased the property. But just two and a half years later, it was for sale again. There have been no reports of ghostly activity there in recent years, but that doesn't mean that the spirits of Marie LaLaurie's victims are resting in peace.

During a remodeling of the LaLaurie Mansion some years ago, workers discovered several unmarked graves under the floorboards of the house. This may explain why many of Marie LaLaurie's slaves simply disappeared, never to be seen again.

The USS *Hornet*: The Spirits of World War II Live On

The USS Hornet *is a floating piece of history. This World War II–era aircraft carrier is as long as three football fields. In its heyday, it housed a hospital, a tailor shop, three barbershops, and seven kitchens. The recipient of nine battle stars for military service, the* Hornet *could carry 3,500 sailors. During World War II, its pilots destroyed 1,410 Japanese aircrafts and almost 1.3 tons of enemy cargo. But in its 27 years of service, the* Hornet *also saw 300 deaths from battles, accidents, and suicides. In fact, this ship is believed to hold the Navy record for the most suicides. If that isn't enough to produce a ghost or two, what is?*

It's a Strange, Strange World

Considered one of the most haunted ships in history, the USS *Hornet* now sits docked at the Alameda Naval Air Station in California. Since completing an illustrious military career, the ship has become a naval museum—and it just happens to be full of ghosts.

Since the *Hornet*'s arrival in Alameda, tourists and staff members have noticed some very strange things aboard the old ship. In fact, several websites are devoted to reporting weird happenings on the *Hornet,* all of which are noted by regular people who just happen to experience them. Many witnesses who were skeptics now believe in ghosts.

The paranormal activity on the USS *Hornet* includes unusual noises, items that come up missing, and apparitions. Psychics and ghost hunters who have investigated the abnormal occurrences there agree that the ship's spirits are probably the souls of departed sailors who died abruptly. Perhaps they're still trying to carry out their final orders.

Many visitors on the ship report feeling that someone touched or grabbed them when no one else was in sight. There's no need to be afraid, though, because almost all accounts describe friendly spirits. In fact, many of the ghosts—which are primarily men—are quite the pranksters. And oddly, not all of them seem to be navy men. Members of other branches of the military have also been spotted on board dressed in their respective uniforms.

No place is off limits to these free spirits. Those who have seen the ghostly figures on the ship say that they look so real that they blend in with the living. They appear dressed in uniform, patrolling the hallways and performing their shipboard duties. They've also been spotted on decks, in bathrooms, climbing ladders, and in the Combat Information Center. Toilets mysteriously flush by themselves, lights turn on and off on their own, and men are heard talking in areas where no one else appears to be present.

The Spirits of World War II

The steam room is one of the most haunted sections of the USS *Hornet.* That's probably because it was one of the most dangerous areas of the ship. The spirit of a sailor who died in the steam room is thought to remain there. Some say that because he died so quickly, he doesn't even realize that he's dead.

Not all the ghosts on the USS *Hornet* are American. One spirit that has appeared to many visitors is that of a Japanese pilot who was a prisoner of war on board the ship during World War II. He supposedly went crazy and died in the small cell where he was kept. His restless spirit still inhabits that room—and he's still trying to get out.

Another ghost that has been seen on the ship quite often is that of Admiral Joseph "Jocko" Clark, who served as the vessel's commander during World War II. After calling the *Hornet* home for so many years, it seems that his spirit may have sought out the place where he felt most at home. Even decades after his passing, it appears that he's still married to the sea.

The Ghosts of Gettysburg

The Battle of Gettysburg holds an interesting yet tragic place in American history. It was the turning point of the Civil War. It was also its bloodiest battle. From July 1 through July 3, 1863, the Union and Confederate armies suffered a total of more than 50,000 casualties (dead, wounded, and missing) on the battlefields of Gettysburg, Pennsylvania. All that bloodshed and suffering is said to have permanently stained the town and left it overflowing with ghosts. Not surprisingly, Gettysburg is often named one of the most haunted places in America.

First Ghost Sighting

Did you know that the first sighting of a ghost at Gettysburg allegedly took place *before* the battle was even over? As the story goes, Union troops from the 20th Maine Infantry were nearing Gettysburg, but they got lost as they traveled in the dark. As the troops marched on, they were greeted by a man wearing a tricornered hat, who was sitting on top of a horse. Both the man and his horse appeared to be glowing. The man, who bore a striking resemblance to George Washington, motioned for the troops to follow. Believing that the man was a Union general, Colonel Joshua Chamberlain ordered his men to do so. But just as Chamberlain began to think that something was odd about the helpful fellow, the man simply vanished.

As the soldiers searched for the spectral stranger, they realized that they'd been led to Little Round Top. This location is now famous because the following day, the Union troops held off a Confederate advance in one of the turning points of the battle. To his dying day, Chamberlain, as well as the roughly 100 men who saw the ghostly figure that night, believed that they had been led to Little Round Top by the ghost of George Washington himself.

Pickett's Charge

On the final day of the Battle of Gettysburg, Confederate General Robert E. Lee felt the chance of victory slipping away from him. So, in what many saw as a desperate act, he ordered 12,000 Confederate soldiers to attack the Union forces that were settled on a hill known as Cemetery Ridge. During the attack that is now known as Pickett's Charge, the Confederates slowly and methodically marched across open fields toward the heavily armed Union lines. The attack failed miserably. More than 6,000 Confederate soldiers were killed or wounded before they retreated. The defeat essentially signaled the beginning of the end of the Civil War.

To this day, it is said that if you stand atop Cemetery Ridge and look out across the field, you might catch a glimpse of row after ghostly row of Confederate soldiers slowly marching toward their doom at the hands of Union troops.

Jennie Wade

While the battle raged near Cemetery Ridge, 20-year-old Mary Virginia "Jennie" Wade was at her sister's house baking bread for the Union troops stationed nearby. Without warning, a stray bullet flew through the house, struck the young woman, and killed her instantly. She was the only civilian known to have died during the Battle of Gettysburg. Visitors to the historic Jennie Wade House often report catching whiffs of freshly baked bread. Jennie's spirit is also felt in the basement, where her body was placed until her family could bury her. When the TV show *Ghost Lab* visited the Jennie Wade House in 2010, phantom footsteps were heard and other evidence was captured on audio recorders.

Farnsworth House

Although it is next to impossible to determine who fired the shot that killed Jennie Wade, it is believed that it came from the attic of the nearby Farnsworth House. The building is now a bed-and-breakfast, but during the Battle of Gettysburg, it was taken over by Confederate snipers. One in particular—the one who may have fired the shot that killed Jennie Wade—is said to have holed up in the building's attic. He didn't survive the battle, but judging by the dozens of bullet holes and scars along the sides of the Farnsworth House, he didn't go down without a fight. Perhaps that's why his ghost still lingers—to let us know what really happened in the Farnsworth attic. People passing by often report looking up at the attic window that faces the Jennie Wade House and seeing a ghostly figure peering down at them.

But the sniper is just one of many spirits that haunt the Farnsworth House. Paranormal experts claim that the home features no less than 14 ghosts; some are friendly, and some are not. Representing the friendly, "Mary" sits beside the sick and lingers wherever there's cheering up to be done. It is believed that this compassionate phantom was a nurse or midwife during her mortal years.

Then there's "Walter." He's the complete opposite of Mary. It is believed that he was a Confederate soldier who was jilted by his girlfriend before being killed. Maybe that's why Walter's ghost seems determined to get revenge on women. Reports state that a female guest was once attacked by an invisible presence. Another time, an unseen force hurled a chair at a female visitor. Many people blame Walter for both incidents.

Pennsylvania Hall at Gettysburg College

Built in 1832, Gettysburg College stands near the famous battlefield. During the conflict, some of its buildings served as operating rooms and makeshift morgues. Late one night in the early 1980s, two college administrators got on an elevator and pushed the button to go down to the first floor. But the elevator went past the first floor and continued to the basement, where the doors opened. It didn't take long for the workers to realize that they'd somehow traveled back in time. The familiar surroundings of the basement had been replaced by bloody screaming Confederate soldiers on stretchers. Doctors stood over the men, desperately trying to save their lives. Blood and gore were everywhere.

As the administrators frantically pushed the elevator buttons, one of the spectral doctors began walking toward them. Without a second to spare, the elevator doors closed just as the ghostly figure reached them. This time, the elevator rose to the first floor and opened its doors, revealing modern furnishings. Despite repeated return visits to the basement, nothing out of the ordinary has ever been reported again.

Spend the Night with a Ghost at One of These Hotels

By their very nature, hotels would have a lot to say if their walls could talk. So many travelers passing through, so many stories—and so many ghosts left behind. Hotels provide their guests with soft beds and hearty breakfasts, but if your hotel happens to be haunted, you may get a little more with your room than you expected.

The Heathman Hotel (Portland, Oregon)

Guests should choose their rooms at the Heathman Hotel carefully because there's a certain column of rooms that reportedly sees quite a bit of paranormal action. Pick rooms ending in 03 (between 303 and 1003) only if you don't mind spending the night with a ghostly companion. George Heathman built the hotel in 1927 for lumber and railroad tycoons who sought luxurious lodging in the West. No one knows what actually caused the hauntings, but ghost hunters think that someone fell or jumped out of a window and now haunts the rooms that he or she passed on the way down. Today, guests in those rooms experience odd occurrences, such as towels being used and glasses and chairs being moved when no one else has been in the room. Visitors have also felt a strange presence in some rooms. One guest even woke up to find himself wrapped up tightly in his sheets.

Hotel Vendome (Prescott, Arizona)

Prescott is a quaint and welcoming community in the Arizona mountains, and the town holds a lot of history. Former manager Abby Byr and her cat, Noble, are said to haunt this hotel, which was built in 1917. At around that same time, Abby, who suffered from tuberculosis, moved to Arizona for health reasons. There, she met and married her husband, and the couple bought the Hotel Vendome. They soon lost the place due to unpaid taxes, but the next owners hired them to run it. One night in 1921, Abby sent her husband out for medicine, but he never returned. She died a short time later, and employees, guests, and ghost hunters have all felt her presence lingering at the hotel. Some have even seen her ghost in Room 16, where she and her husband lived. Is it Abby who makes noise by moving hangers around in the closet? Guests have also reported having their things inexplicably moved around the room, and some report getting sudden whiffs of strong perfume.

Fairmont Hotel Vancouver (Vancouver, British Columbia)

Opened in 1939, the Fairmont Hotel is still going strong today. Adding to the hotel's distinguished architecture and fabulous ambience are a few ghostly spirits. Over the years, guests and employees have reported seeing a spectral Lady in Red that roams the hallways of the 14th floor and sometimes appears to walk along an invisible ledge. Also, elevators have been known to make unscheduled stops on the 14th floor, even though the button was not pressed and no one is there when the door opens.

Jerome Grand Hotel (Jerome, Arizona)

Jerome, Arizona, got its start as a mining town in the late 1800s. In the late 1920s, the United Verde Copper Company built a hospital there to treat sick and injured miners. In addition to the many deaths that are typically associated with a hospital, several violent ones occurred in the building as well. In 1935, an orderly was found crushed beneath the elevator, and another fell from a fifth-floor balcony. Both deaths are thought to have been murders. A suicide also took place at the hospital when a patient rolled his wheelchair over a balcony and onto the street below.

The hospital closed its doors in 1950 and the building sat vacant for nearly half a century until two brothers opened the Jerome Grand Hotel there in 1997. The third floor has seen the most paranormal activity, but disembodied voices and coughing, a dusty smell, and apparitions have been reported throughout the building. They're most likely the antics of spirits left over from the days when the sick and injured lived and died there.

Fairmont Château Laurier (Ottawa, Ontario)

The spirits of this hotel are evidence that ghosts from the *Titanic* do not just haunt the ship and its artifacts. In 1912, Charles Melville Hays journeyed to Europe to choose dining-room furniture for the Château Laurier. Unfortunately, he and his men went down with the *Titanic* just days before the hotel was scheduled to open. However, Hays's spirit is believed to have returned to the Château Laurier, where guests report objects that have moved by themselves and walls that shake and rattle—just like on a topsy-turvy ship.

Landmark Inn (Marquette, Michigan)

A certain fascination surrounds sailors and their lives on the water. In the 1930s, shortly after the Landmark Inn first opened its doors, a local librarian fell in love with a sailor on leave from his ship on Lake Superior. He planned one last trip before returning to marry her, but neither the sailor nor his ship ever returned. The librarian died of a broken heart a short time later. She is thought to haunt the Landmark Inn's

Lilac Room, where her apparition looks out over the lake, awaiting the return of her lost love. Men who have stayed in this room have reported having tricks played on them. Their keys don't always work in the lock, objects are moved around the room, and they receive phone calls in the middle of the night—with no one on the other end. The hotel's front desk has also received phone calls *from* the Lilac Room when the room was empty.

Pfister Hotel (Milwaukee, Wisconsin)

Professional sports teams like to psych out their opponents, but putting them up in a haunted hotel might be a bit extreme! Actually, the elegant Pfister Hotel in downtown Milwaukee has all the amenities that professional baseball and basketball players appreciate. The ghosts are just a bonus.

The specter of hotel founder Charles Pfister is thought to look out over the grand staircase to make sure that guests are well cared for. Other spirits have been noted near the ballroom, and odd noises are heard in several of the guest rooms. Former major-league baseball manager Tony La Russa said that guests get first-class service at the Pfister, and if there happen to be a few ghosts, "they're good friends." But just to be safe, some baseball players always request to share rooms when they're in Milwaukee. One even sleeps with his baseball bat when his team stays at the Pfister!

These Haunted Libraries Contain More Than Just Spooky Stories

In the classic movie Ghostbusters *(1984), a team of paranormal investigators encounters the ghost of an elderly woman reading a book while floating amongst the shelves at the New York Public Library. When they speak to her, she shushes them. After all, libraries are supposed to be quiet places—even ghosts respect that rule! But the team continues its work, which causes the sweet specter to transform into an evil entity. Think that only happens in the movies? The following haunted libraries may make you think again.*

A. B. Safford Memorial Library (Cairo, Illinois)

Resident spirit "Toby" likes to hang out on the second floor of the A. B. Safford Memorial Library. Staff members have heard his footsteps at night, and he's been blamed for the creaking noises that a rocking chair makes even when no one is in it and it's not moving. Toby has also been known to switch lights on and off. And library employees once witnessed a "ghostly light" emerge from behind a desk and travel down a hall before vanishing in the bookshelves.

Hutchinson Public Library (Hutchinson, Kansas)

After librarian Ida Day Holzapfel died in 1954, she began to hang around her former place of employment, the Hutchinson Public Library. One day in 1975, a librarian saw a strange woman hovering below the stairs. When she described what she'd seen to a coworker, she was told it was Holzapfel. Footsteps and disembodied voices have been heard in the basement, and some witnesses have glimpsed Holzapfel's apparition hanging around by the bookshelves.

Millicent Library (Fairhaven, Massachusetts)

In 1893, Henry Huttleston Rogers founded the Millicent Library, which he named for his daughter, who had died at age 17. Bathed in blue light, Millicent walks the halls during the day and stands in a window at night. But apparently, she's not alone. Witnesses have also seen a woman dressed in black running her fingers along the books. And a man wearing a purple bow tie, a tweed jacket, and small round glasses has been spotted mopping the basement floor.

New Hanover County Public Library (Wilmington, North Carolina)

A ghost that is apparently obsessed with researching the Civil War spends a lot of time in the North Carolina Room at the New Hanover County Public Library. On several occasions, librarians have come to work in the morning to find files scattered on a table despite the fact that everything was put away the night before. People have also heard the rustling of pages turning even though they are alone. And once, the glass door of a locked bookcase began shaking violently on its own.

Easton Area Public Library (Easton, Pennsylvania)

The Easton Area Public Library might be the most haunted library in the United States. When the Carnegie Foundation offered Easton $50,000 to build a public library if the town would contribute the land, the most suitable site was already occupied by an old cemetery. The grounds were cleared, and most of the graves were relocated, but some were moved to a vault that is now located underneath the back exit of the library's parking lot. The graves of William Parsons, the founder of Easton, and Elizabeth "Mammy" Bell Morgan, who ran a local hotel, are still located there.

Since the library opened in 1903, articles in the local newspaper have reported that it is haunted. Some people have claimed to see a lady with a glowing head floating in a window. Others have witnessed a headless woman wandering the grounds and glowing lights traveling throughout the building.

Sweetwater County Library (Green River, Wyoming)

It's not surprising that the Sweetwater County Library is haunted. After all, it's built on the site of a graveyard. Since the mid-1980s, lights have mysteriously turned on and off by themselves, and orbs of light have been known to move along the walls inside the art gallery, even when it's empty. Strange flapping sounds are heard throughout the building at night, and two old electric typewriters once began operating on their own. The paranormal activity at the library is so common that in 1993, staff members started a "Ghost Log" to document their experiences.

A Voice from Beyond the Grave

After the murder of Teresita Basa in the late 1970s, another woman began to speak in Teresita's voice. The voice said things that only Teresita could have known . . . like who killed her.

In February 1977, firemen broke into a burning apartment on North Pine Grove Avenue in Chicago. Beneath a pile of burning clothes, they found the body of 47-year-old Teresita Basa, a hospital worker who was said to be a member of the Filipino aristocracy. There were bruises on her neck and a kitchen knife was lodged in her chest.

Unfortunately, the police were left without a single lead. They had no suspects and no apparent motive for the brutal murder. The solution would come from the strangest of all possible sources—a voice from beyond the grave.

"I Am Teresita Basa"

Remibios Chua lived just outside of Chicago in the town of Evanston. Shortly after Teresita's death, Remibios started going into trances during which she spoke in Tagalog, a language used in the Philippines. In a slow, clear voice,

Remibios said, “I am Teresita Basa.” Although Remibios had worked at the same hospital as Teresita, they didn’t know each other. Remibios’s husband, Dr. Jose Chua, had never heard of Teresita either.

When Remibios came out of the trances, she remembered very little, if anything, about what she had said. But while speaking in the mysterious voice, she claimed that Teresita’s killer was a man named Allan Showery. He was also an employee at the hospital where both women had worked. She stated that he had killed Teresita while stealing jewelry for rent money.

Through Remibios’s lips, the voice begged them to contact the police. The frightened couple initially resisted, fearing that the authorities would think that *they* should be locked away. But when the voice returned and continued pleading for an investigation, the Chuas finally contacted the police. Detective Joe Stachula was assigned to the case.

Lacking any other clues, Stachula interviewed the Chuas. During their conversation, Remibios not only named the killer, but she also told Stachula exactly where to find the jewelry that Showery had allegedly stolen from Teresita. Prior to that, the police were not even aware that anything had been taken from Teresita’s apartment.

Remarkably, when police began investigating Showery, they found his girlfriend in possession of Teresita’s jewelry.

Although the authorities declined to list the voice from beyond the grave as evidence, Showery was arrested, and he initially confessed to the crime. When his lawyers learned that information leading to his arrest had come from supernatural sources, they advised him to take back his confession.

The Surprise Confession

Not surprisingly, the voice became a focal point of the case when it went to trial in January 1979. The defense called the Chuas to the witness stand in an effort to prove that the entire case against Showery was based on remarks made by a woman who claimed to be possessed—hardly the sort of evidence that would hold up in court.

But the prosecution argued that no matter the origin of the voice, it had turned out to be correct. In his closing statement, prosecuting attorney Thomas Organ said, "Did Teresita Basa come back from the dead and name Showery? I don't know. I'm a skeptic, but it doesn't matter as to guilt or innocence. What does matter is that the information furnished to police checked out. The jewelry was found where the voice said it would be found, and Showery confessed."

Detective Stachula was asked if he believed the Chuas: "I would not call anyone a liar," he said. "... Dr. and Mrs. Chua are educated, intelligent people.... I listened and acted on what they told me... [and] the case was wrapped up within three hours."

Showery told the jury that he was "just kidding" when he confessed to the crime. He also claimed that the police had coerced him into an admission of guilt. Nevertheless, after 13 hours of deliberation, the jury reported that they were hopelessly deadlocked and a mistrial was declared.

In a shocking development a few weeks later, Allan Showery changed his plea to "guilty." He was eventually sentenced to 14 years in prison. Some say that Teresita's ghost had visited him and frightened him into confessing.

The Chuas were obviously shaken by the experience, so they avoided the press as much as possible. In 1980, in her only interview with the press, Remibios said that during the trial, people were afraid to ride in cars with her. But she said that she was never afraid because the voice said that God would protect her family. Still, she hoped that she would never have to go through such an experience again. "I've done my job," she said. "I don't think I will ever want to go through this same ordeal."

Having attracted national attention, the case quickly became the subject of a best-selling book and countless magazine articles, a TV movie, and a 1990 episode of *Unsolved Mysteries*. The case is often cited as "proof" of psychic phenomena, possession, and ghosts, but it's simply another mystery of the paranormal world. Exactly what it proves is impossible to say. After all, the ghost of Teresita Basa is no longer talking.

Lincoln's Ghost Train

Abraham Lincoln's funeral train appears to have been much like the president himself: uncommonly determined and larger than life.

Final Journey

When President Lincoln was assassinated in April 1865, the nation was understandably plunged into a state of mourning. Swept away was the "Great Emancipator," who had not only put an end to slavery but had also preserved a war-torn nation. For everything that he had done for the country, it was decided that Lincoln's funeral procession should be as great as the man himself. In order to bring the president close to the citizens who loved and mourned him, his funeral train would trace the same route—in reverse—that Lincoln had traveled when he went to Washington, D.C., four years earlier as president-elect. Covering a vast 1,654 miles, the train left Washington on April 21, 1865, and finally pulled into Springfield, Illinois, on May 3. Officially, this was Lincoln's last ride—but unofficially, some say that Abe and his funeral train have never stopped chugging along.

First Phantom

In April 1866, one year after Lincoln's assassination, the first report of the ghost train surfaced. The sighting occurred along a stretch of railway in New York's Hudson Valley. Witnesses told a fantastic tale of a phantom train that whooshed by them without making a sound. They identified it as Lincoln's funeral train because they saw the president's flag-draped coffin on board. Surrounded by black fabric, the casket was identical to the original but with one notable difference. This time, a *skeletal* honor guard stood at attention beside it. Witnesses also recalled seeing an equally skeletal band. But it seemed rather bizarre that no sounds came from their musical instruments.

A strange bluish light surrounded the train as it chugged silently northward. Witnesses said that a blast of warm air could be felt and that clocks inexplicably stopped for six

minutes as the train slowly passed by. Over time, this vision would be reported surprisingly often along much of the original train's route.

Mass Hysteria?

With such a huge tragedy, it was almost a given that sightings of Lincoln's ghost would occur. Psychologists attribute such phenomena to denial—the subconscious act of refusing to let go. Lincoln had restored peace to a nation whose future had hung delicately in the balance. It seemed extremely unfair that he should be taken away in such a brutal fashion. And yet, he had been.

Still, what can be said of a phantom train that appears to numerous people along so vast a route? While shock and denial might account for individual sightings of a spectral president, it seems doubtful that an entire funeral train could be imagined by scores of people at precisely the same time. And how could the details of such sightings match so closely from person to person and region to region?

Just Passing Through

If witnesses are to be believed, Lincoln's ghost train still chugs along on its seemingly endless journey. Sightings of it generally occur in April, the month in which the original funeral train began its trek. Details of eyewitness accounts are surprisingly similar to each other. But a few differences have been reported. Some people say that the ghost train contains several cars that are all draped in black. Others say that it only consists of an engine and one flatbed car that holds the dead president's coffin. And every so often, someone claims to hear a shrieking whistle coming from the phantom locomotive.

Despite such detailed accounts, naysayers exist. In his book *The Lincoln Funeral Train,* author Scott Trostel discusses his belief that these accounts are simply the products of people's "vivid and fertile imaginations." Perhaps, but how is it that different people in different states have such similar vivid and fertile imaginations? Like Lincoln himself, the question belongs to the ages.

Tormented Spirits at the Lizzie Borden Bed & Breakfast

Lizzie Borden took an ax
And gave her mother 40 whacks.
And when she saw what she had done,
She gave her father 41.

This poem has been a schoolyard staple for more than a century, but it's actually incorrect. First, it states that Lizzie Borden whacked her mother with an ax 40 times before turning on her father. In reality, the Bordens were murdered with a hatchet, not an ax. And Mrs. Borden suffered around

20 wounds while her husband suffered 11—still more than enough to kill them both. What's more, Abby Borden was Lizzie's stepmother, not her mother.

But the poem may have yet another error: Lizzie Borden may not have been the killer at all!

"Father's Dead!"

Lizzie Borden grew up in Fall River, Massachusetts. In 1892, when the murders took place, Lizzie was still single and living at home at age 32, even though most women were married by their late teens or early twenties back then.

On August 4, 1892, the family's maid, Bridget Sullivan, was in her upstairs room when she heard Lizzie screaming. "Come down quick!" Lizzie shouted. "Father's dead! Someone's come in and killed him!"

Andrew Borden was lying dead on the couch, the victim of multiple hatchet wounds. By some accounts, he had been rolled over to look like he was merely sleeping, but there was blood everywhere.

While neighbors tended to the shocked Lizzie, she was asked where she had been when all of this happened. She told them that she had gone to the barn to get something.

A little while later, the police found the body of Abby Borden in a guest room. She was even more mutilated than Andrew.

Lizzie was the only person who the police ever arrested for the crime. There had been a great deal of tension between Lizzie and her father, for a variety of reasons. For example, Andrew's decision to will his property to his relatives, rather than divide it among his children, had caused much strife within the family. Also, he had recently killed Lizzie's pet pigeons, which he said had become a nuisance. He decapitated them and left the bodies for Lizzie to find.

Not long before the murders, Andrew had suspected that he was being poisoned. But he didn't know who to accuse. After all, he was very unpopular in town because of his miserly ways and shrewd business dealings. The culprit could have been almost anyone! But few people get poisoned simply for being unpopular. Besides, Lizzie had been spotted buying cyanide at a local pharmacy just days before the murders. This made her look fairly suspicious.

In addition, Lizzie's explanation that she had been in the barn while the murders took place didn't convince everyone. For one thing, the bodies looked like they'd been moved. And how long could it possibly have taken her to get something out of the barn?

The Verdict

Although the evidence against her was slim, Lizzie was arrested for the murders. There were no bloodstains on her dress when the police arrived on the scene, and no bloody clothes were ever found. A broken hatchet was located in the basement, but it could not be connected to the murders. With no solid evidence against Lizzie, the jury deliberated just 90 minutes before setting her free.

After the trial, Lizzie changed her name to "Lizbeth" and went on with her life. She moved to a new home and lived a somewhat lavish lifestyle until her death in 1927.

Today, there are dozens of theories about the identity of the actual killer. Some say that it *was* Lizzie, while others think that it wasn't her but that she knew very well who it was. Still others believe that Lizzie had nothing to do with it. The sad truth is that we'll probably never know for sure who committed the crime. But the ghosts of Andrew and Abby Borden may want to keep the investigation alive.

Can You Still Hear the Screams?

The Borden House is now a museum/bed-and-breakfast that is made to look almost exactly like it did at the time of the murders. Guests can actually sleep in the very room where Abby Borden was killed and eat a breakfast of bananas, coffee, and johnnycakes (flattened cornbread), just like

Mr. and Mrs. Borden did on that fateful morning before their brutal deaths.

Ghost sightings in the old green Victorian house are common. MSNBC even listed the house among the top ten most haunted houses in the United States.

The most active ghost there seems to be that of Abby Borden. Many guests have reported hearing the sound of a woman weeping in the bedroom where Abby's body was found. Many others have heard the sound of footsteps. And some people have even reported that as they lay in their beds, an older woman in an old-fashioned dress came into the room to tuck them in for the night.

But Abby is not the only ghost that roams the B and B. Guests have also occasionally spotted Andrew. He has also manifested during séances that have been held at the house.

Lizzie's spirit has also been seen at the Borden home. From time to time, guests see a ghostly woman carrying a sharp weapon. Could this be Lizzie—or is it the *real* murderer?

Whoever they are, the ghosts at the Lizzie Borden Bed & Breakfast certainly aren't shy. Many guests have captured strange photos, videos, and audio recordings that feature unusual blobs of light, sounds resembling screams, and shadows that simply shouldn't be there. The owner of the house admits to being touched and pushed by unseen hands.

In 2008, a couple visiting on the anniversary of the murders fled the B and B in terror after the door to their room flung open by itself and a lamp moved and lit up on its own.

There are many haunted hotels around the world, but few generate as much paranormal activity as the Lizzie Borden Bed & Breakfast. Allegedly, the Bordens don't just haunt their former home. People have seen mysterious lights at Oak Grove Cemetery, where the family is buried. And a few folks have even heard screams coming from the Borden plot, where Lizzie's body lies right next to the remains of her father and stepmother.

Ghosts Live On at the Clovis Sanitarium

Picture this scene at the emergency call center in Clovis, California: "Hello. 911. What's your emergency?" Dead silence. "Hello? Is anyone there?" More silence. So the dispatcher checks to see where the call is coming from. It's coming from 2604 Clovis Avenue, the former home of the Clovis Sanitarium—a building that has no electricity and no working phone. It's probably not a life-or-death situation, since whomever is making the call is already dead.

Oddly, this type of phone call is not uncommon in Clovis—a city of 95,000 that is located just northeast of Fresno. Clovis was the home of Anthony Andriotti, who built a magnificent mansion for his family in 1922. Unfortunately, he miscalculated the cost of the building's upkeep. He ended up bankrupt and turned to drugs and alcohol. He died in 1929 at age 36.

The estate sat empty until it was reopened in 1935 as the Hazelwood Sanitarium for tuberculosis patients. In 1942, it became the Clovis Avenue Sanitarium, which was dedicated to serving the area's physically and mentally ill.

A Place to Die

Families whose loved ones suffered from the gravest mental illnesses brought those unfortunate souls to the Clovis Sanitarium to die. It is said that at one point, the death rate at the facility reached an average of one person per day. Still, the building soon became overcrowded, with ten beds to a room and one nurse handling two or more rooms. Former employees told sad tales of patients who were abused and neglected.

When patients died, their bodies were stored in the relatively cool basement until they could be removed. Locals started talking about strange happenings at the sanitarium, and rumors began to suggest that the place was haunted. But it wasn't all just gossip. It seems that there *were* some pretty weird things going on at 2604 Clovis Avenue.

A Call for Help

In 1992, the Clovis Sanitarium closed. That's when the mysterious phone calls began. Sometimes neighbors or people passing by would call the police to report trespassers or vandals. But then there were the other calls—the ones that came directly from the vacant building that had no working phone line.

Unfazed by these odd stories, Todd Wolfe bought the property in 1997 with hopes of creating a haunted house attraction for Halloween. In the beginning, Todd didn't believe that the place was haunted. So he was surprised when his employees complained about spirits interfering with their work. They saw apparitions and reported being touched and grabbed by unseen hands. But then, Todd actually saw a shadowy spirit in "Mary's Room." After that, he began to believe. Today, Mary's Room is furnished with only original furniture because it seems that "Mary" gets quite upset when changes are made. And a disturbed Mary leads to increased paranormal activity, including phantom breathing, shoving by an invisible force, and objects that move on their own.

Many paranormal groups have visited the Clovis Sanitarium, and all agree that it is indeed haunted. They've heard shuffling footsteps and strange voices, and many have reported feelings of being watched.

Energetic Spirits

When the *Ghost Adventures* team visited the Clovis Sanitarium to film a 2010 episode, they were greeted by a laughing spirit and a spike in electromagnetic energy (in a building where the electricity is turned off). Later, the crew's state-of-the-art ultraviolet camera recorded a mysterious purple form in the basement. The shape even sat on a couch for a while. The team also captured some amazing EVPs (electronic voice phenomena), including one that told the group to "Get out" and another that said it wanted their energy.

Investigator Zak Bagans observed that the original owners were a family with young children who lived a lavish lifestyle, full of happiness and laughter. But those feelings combined with the hopelessness felt by the mentally ill who were neglected and abused after being brought there to die. As Bagans concluded, "That contrasting energy has to do something weird to the atmosphere."

"There are some human beings who are dimly aware of their own deaths, yet have chosen to stay on in what used to be their homes, to be close to surroundings they once held dear."

—Hans Holzer, famous paranormal researcher

Casper the Friendly Ghost

A friendly ghost so doggone sweet that kids run toward him? What on earth were his creators thinking? Cha-ching! That's what they were thinking.

He's a Scream!

In 1940, Seymour Reit and Joe Oriolo created Casper the Friendly Ghost as a storybook. But it took a few years for Casper to make his first public appearance. That's when Paramount Pictures Famous Studios released Casper not as a book but as part of its animated Noveltoon cartoon series. During his early years, Casper went through some growing pains and even survived a brash suicide attempt. Yikes!

Ghastly Genealogy

Believe it or not, lovable Casper's family tree actually has some pretty dark roots. The very fact that Casper is a ghost suggests that he was once alive but died. But did he? Casper was seen residing beside gravestones in his earliest cartoon strips, but later, he mysteriously grew very humanlike feet and was often seen with his two ghostly parents. Some say that such clues prove his mortality. Others disagree. They believe that Casper and his family were simply "born" as ghosts or were supernatural beings. While no definitive answer exists (fans are still debating Casper's origins), such uncertainty probably sprang from Paramount's concerns over keeping the "Friendly Ghost" friendly—especially to easily startled young viewers. After all, there'd be little sense in making Casper the ghost of a dead child if the goal was *not* to scare the wits out of American youngsters. On the other hand, it's difficult to explain Casper's existence any other way. Some things are just better left unknown.

A Suicidal New Yawker?

It may shock some to learn that Casper began his cartoon career at Paramount as a ghost-child from New York, but this was strongly suggested by his thick accent. It may also be surprising to learn that in "The Friendly Ghost," the very first Casper cartoon short produced by Paramount in 1944, the ghost-boy tried to end his "life" by lying across railroad tracks. Thankfully, because Casper was already a ghost, the train passed right through him. The outcome pleased fans, and it spared writers the task of explaining how a ghost dies again.

Grown-Ups Don't Understand

Perhaps the most memorable part of the Casper experience was the theme song created for the TV cartoon series of the early 1950s. Written by Jerry Livingston and Mack David, the catchy ditty features lyrics that have etched themselves into the minds of children everywhere:

Grown-ups don't understand,
why children love him the most,
but kids all know that he loves them so
Casper, the friendly ghost.

Young Casper fans were eager to jump on the bandwagon, and Casper lunch boxes, board games, Halloween costumes, and stuffed toys sold like hotcakes.

Still Friendly After All These Years

Over the years, Casper has been featured in animated movies and cartoons, comic books, and even a live-action feature film (*Casper,* 1995). It was in this movie that the sweet specter's story was finally told.... Or was it? Viewers learned that he was really a 12-year-old boy named Casper McFadden, who died of pneumonia. But in the follow-up films *Casper: A Spirited Beginning* (1997) and *Casper Meets Wendy* (1998), these ideas are contradicted. With so much conflicting information, we may never fully understand Casper.

RIP RIP RIP RIP

Ghostly Guests Stay for Free at the Hotel del Coronado

If you're like most people, you love to get free stuff, especially during a hotel stay. At the Hotel del Coronado in California, you get all the usual amenities plus the chance to share your room with resident ghost Kate Morgan.

Guests and Ghosts

Any building that dates back to 1888 is certainly rich with history, and the Hotel del Coronado is no exception. For more than a century, travelers—many with stories and secrets of their own—have passed through its elegant doors. This grand structure is perched right next to the Pacific Ocean. When it was built, it was the largest building outside of New York City to feature electric lighting. Today, Coronado, California, is a rather wealthy town, but in the late 1800s, it was filled with crime and corruption. "The Del," as the hotel is nicknamed, offered its guests a peaceful escape where they could relax and forget their troubles. The building was named a National Historic Landmark in 1977, and it is still in operation today.

Over the years, the Del became a vacation hot spot for celebrities and politicians. Marilyn Monroe stayed there while filming *Some Like It Hot* (1959), and author L. Frank Baum is said to have written much of *The Wonderful Wizard of Oz* in his room at the famous hotel. In fact, it is believed that the Emerald City was inspired by the Del's architecture. But the hotel's most notable guest may be Kate Morgan—

a young woman who checked into the Del in November 1892 . . . and never left.

Many stories have been told about Kate Morgan, but most of them agree that the 24-year-old woman checked into Room 302 under the name Lottie Bernard. The beautiful young woman appeared to be either ill or upset, and she had no luggage. She said that she was planning to meet her "brother" for the Thanksgiving holiday, but several days later, she was found on the hotel steps . . . with a bullet in her head. Her death was ruled a suicide.

The Background

The story behind the story is that Kate and her husband, Tom, had been staging a bit of a con game. They traveled the rails setting up card games that Tom invariably won. While Kate pretended to be Tom's sister, she flirted shamelessly with men who tried to impress her with their card-playing skills. She was impressed all right—to the tune of hundreds of dollars.

Kate finally tired of the scheming and the traveling, and like other young women her age, she longed to settle down and start a family. For a brief time, Tom and Kate lived in Los Angeles, but Tom grew restless and headed back out on the rails. Shortly after he left, Kate discovered that she was pregnant. She made the mistake of telling this joyous news to her husband while on a train to San Diego. They argued, and he went on to another city, while she continued to her final destination: the Hotel del Coronado.

Evidence suggests that Kate traveled across the bay to San Diego, where she purchased a gun and some bullets. Those who saw her reported that she seemed pale and sickly. They weren't surprised when she was found dead.

The Spirited Kate

Guests and employees alike have felt Kate's presence in several places around the Del, including her guest room, the beach, and some of the hotel shops. One boutique, known as Established in 1888, has been the site of some particularly unusual activity. A display of Marilyn Monroe memorabilia was often targeted and such items literally flew off the shelves. Staff members came to the conclusion that Kate was jealous of the famous actress. When the Marilyn souvenirs were moved to a corner and replaced with mugs, both areas settled down and no more unusual activity was reported.

An apparition dressed in a long black dress has been seen around the shop and in the hallways. And a maintenance man at the hotel reports that there is one light on the property that will never stay lit—the one over the steps where Kate's lifeless body was found.

The most notable haunting is in the room where Kate stayed in 1892. The room number has since changed from 302 to 3312, and recently to 3327. Room 3502 is thought to be haunted as well. Strange, unexplained events have occurred in both rooms. Guests staying in these rooms have reported toilets flushing by themselves, lights flickering on and off, curtains blowing when the windows are closed, and a lingering floral scent. Ashtrays have been seen flying through the air, temperatures mysteriously go up and down, and televisions blare one minute and are silent the next. Several visitors have also witnessed a ghostly figure standing by the window of Kate's room. And a strange glow has been seen just inside that window from the outside. Hotel guests have reported hearing soft murmurs coming from inside the room. Is it the ocean . . . or the sound of a young woman reliving her sadness and distress over and over again?

Room 3519 at the Del is also thought to be haunted, perhaps even more so than Kate's room. In 1983, a Secret Service agent stayed in Room 3519 while guarding then–Vice President George H. W. Bush. The agent bolted from the room in the middle of the night claiming that he'd heard unearthly gurgling noises and that the entire room seemed to glow.

The Weeping Woman in Gray

If you ever find yourself at Camp Chase Confederate Cemetery in Columbus, Ohio, find the grave of Benjamin F. Allen and listen very closely. If you hear the faint sound of a woman crying, you're in the presence of the cemetery's Lady in Gray.

Camp Chase served as a prison for Confederate officers during the Civil War. But as 1863 dawned, Camp Chase held approximately 8,000 men of every rank.

The sheer number of prisoners soon overwhelmed Camp Chase. Men were forced to share bunks, and shortages of food, clothing, medicine, and other necessities were common. Under those conditions, the prisoners were vulnerable to disease and malnutrition, which led to many deaths. In one particular month alone, 500 men died due to an outbreak of smallpox. Eventually, a cemetery was established at the camp to handle the large number of bodies.

Although Camp Chase was closed shortly after the war, the cemetery remains. Today, it contains the graves of more than 2,100 Confederate soldiers. Although restless spirits are commonly found where miserable deaths occurred, just one ghost is known to call Camp Chase its "home haunt": the famous Lady in Gray. Dressed in a flowing gray dress with a veil hiding her face, she is often seen standing and sobbing over Benjamin Allen's grave. At other times, she can be found weeping at the grave of an unidentified soldier. Occasionally, she leaves flowers on the tombstones.

The Lady in Gray has also been spotted walking among the many gravestones in the cemetery. She's even been seen passing right through the locked cemetery gates. No one knows who she was in life, but some think that she may have been Benjamin Allen's wife. However, her attention to the grave of the unknown soldier baffles researchers. One thing seems certain, though: As long as the Camp Chase Confederate Cemetery exists, the Lady in Gray will watch over it.

Why Are Colleges So Haunted?

Anyone who is familiar with the paranormal can tell you that certain places seem to attract more spirits than others. Colleges and universities are near the top of that list. Are these reports really ghosts? Are they poltergeists? Or are they simply urban legends?

The Poltergeist Profile

Poltergeists are noisy spirits that feed off human energy. They like to get attention by being disruptive, perhaps by throwing objects or moving them around. The reason for this is unclear, but poltergeists tend to manifest around young people between the ages of 8 and 25. In fact, many reported poltergeist cases involve young women between the ages of 14 and 19.

Poltergeists seem attracted to people with dramatic, outgoing personalities. And what better place to find that sort of energy—in ample supply—than at a university?

Ghosts of Students Passed

The college years are some of the best times of many people's lives. But they are also times of growth and change that can be filled with sadness and anxiety. College students often find—and lose—their first loves. They deal with being away from home and struggle to achieve good grades. Unfortunately, due to all this emotion and energy, suicides happen, as do accidents involving alcohol, driving, and domestic violence. Paranormal experts will tell you that it's these types of violent and unexpected deaths that leave spirits earthbound. They may be seeking a do-over, searching for something (or someone) that they can't bear to leave behind, or haunting someone that they couldn't stand in life.

Uneasiness, eerie feelings, the idea that something is just not right—these are all parts of residual hauntings that result from dynamic, violent, or intensely emotional events that have taken place at a certain site. This type of haunting is not the work of one specific ghost but rather the "imprint" of all the emotion and energy that has been spent there. And with all the youthful energy that's crammed onto college campuses, it's easy to see why they are so haunted.

Dream Weaver

John William Dunne was an aeronautical engineer and author of books about paranormal phenomena. He questioned a lot of things in life but nothing more so than dreams and their meanings. His obsession with the twilight world was sparked by an odd event that he couldn't explain. How had he been able to "see" one of the world's greatest tragedies while he was sleeping? And how could this have occurred before the event took place?

J. W. Dunne is best known for the invention of the first practical and stable tailless airplane. But in addition to his aeronautic accomplishments, Dunne presented some important theories about the structure of time in his book *An Experiment with Time.* His interest in this area was prompted by his uncanny knack for forecasting events through his dreams. Of these, one proved particularly mind-boggling.

On the chance that there might be something to his nocturnal visions, Dunne recorded each dream in writing. In early May 1902, while working as an engineer for the British military in South Africa, Dunne had a dream in which he found himself on the island of Martinique. In his vision, the island exploded and some 30,000 people died as a result. Waking up in a cold sweat, Dunne weighed his options. Should he warn the authorities? Or would his amazing claim fall upon deaf ears? Dunne chose to alert the powers that be, but he was unable to persuade them to evacuate the island.

A few days after he had his vision, Dunne received a newspaper at his outpost. To his absolute horror, he discovered that his chilling dream had become a reality. Mount Pelée, located on the island of Martinique, had erupted with unbelievable force. In its wake, around 30,000 people lay dead. Had Dunne foreseen the future, or are the past, present, and future simply imaginary human concepts? The question would preoccupy Dunne for the rest of his waking days—and many of his dream-filled nights, too.

Can Dogs See Ghosts?

It's late at night and you're lying in bed watching TV with your faithful pooch snoring softly at your feet. Suddenly and without warning, your dog bolts upright and looks into the darkened hallway, growling while the hair on the back of his neck stands up. You gather up the courage to investigate, but you find nothing, which leads you to wonder, "Did my dog just see a ghost?"

What Are You Looking At?

In order to know if dogs can see spirits, we must first decide what a ghost looks like. By most accounts, apparitions appear as dark shadows or white, misty shapes that are often only briefly visible out of the corner of one's eye. Sometimes, people report ghosts as glowing balls of light (orbs) that move or dart around. In most cases, they are reported in low-light conditions, which is why many ghost hunters use night-vision cameras when they shoot video or take photographs. So to sum up, if dogs are able to see ghosts, they would need to be able to see:

- Dark shadows or white, misty shapes
- Moving balls of light
- In low light

How a Dog Sees

Just like a human's eye, a dog's eye is made up of rods and cones. Rods function well in low light and are also helpful in detecting movement. Cones help to define colors. Unlike a human eye, the center of a dog's eye is made up mainly of rods, so dogs can't see colors very well. But because apparitions are usually described as dark shadows or white shapes, dogs should be able to see them just fine.

The rods in dogs' eyes allow them to detect motion and see things like flickering lights better than humans can. So if ghosts appear as flitting lights that move quickly, dogs should be able to see them.

Finally, those additional rods in the center of dogs' eyes make it possible for canines to see much better than humans in low-light situations. So while humans scramble for flashlights and night-vision cameras to try to see ghosts, dogs only have to use their eyes.

A Dog's-Eye View

Another thing to consider is the dog's viewpoint. Most adults spend the majority of their time viewing the world from a standing position—typically, more than five feet off the ground. But dogs spend most of their lives looking up at things from about two feet off the ground. That doesn't sound like a big difference, but it is. Just lie on the floor at night and look up at some objects. It really gives you an interesting perspective. Maybe that different viewpoint is what's needed to see spirits.

Refusing to Conform

Finally, remember that dogs don't know that they're not supposed to see ghosts because they allegedly don't exist. So it would stand to reason that a dog, upon seeing an apparition, would simply think that it's seeing a living, breathing person, unlike many skeptical humans who would immediately try to convince themselves that they did not just see a ghost.

RIP RIP RIP RIP

"The boundaries which divide life from death are at best shadowy and vague. Who shall say where the one ends and the other begins."

—Edgar Allan Poe, "The Premature Burial"

FRIGHTENING FACTS

- *In September 1932, actress Peg Entwistle climbed to the top of the Hollywood sign's H and leaped to her death. Since then, a sad spectral blonde in 1930s-era clothing has been spotted there on numerous occasions.*

- *Before Harry Houdini died, he promised to try to contact his family and friends from the afterlife. He and his wife even had a secret code so she would know that it was really him. But he was unable to communicate with his loved ones during multiple séances after his death. However, subsequent residents of his former apartment say that they've seen his apparition there.*

- *La Residencia nursing home in Santa Fe, New Mexico, was once home to St. Vincent Hospital. Years ago, a young boy died there in Room 311 after a car accident, which also claimed the life of his father. The muffled sounds of the boy crying were heard so often that staff members hesitated to assign anyone to that room.*

- *Legendary Civil War photographer Mathew Brady once had a studio near St. Paul's Chapel in Manhattan. In life, Brady loved the city—so much so that he's been unable to leave it. More than a century has passed since his death, but people continue to see his ghost roaming around the area. He is recognizable by his pointed goatee and the distinctive slouch hat that he wears.*

Popping His Top: The Seaford Poltergeist

Poltergeists like to be the center of attention. Other ghosts are happy to lurk in the shadows and then vanish so that nobody's ever exactly sure what they saw. But poltergeist activities are always very flashy and out in the open. Need some furniture rearranged or doors opened or slammed shut? How about knickknacks moved around or plates smashed? If so, just ask a poltergeist. They love to perform such mischief in plain sight. Poltergeists don't care—they just enjoy annoying (and scaring) the living.

Pop! Pop! Pop!

The science of studying poltergeist activity has come a long way since the days when people blamed it all on witchcraft. One of the cases that got folks thinking that there might be more to it was the Seaford Poltergeist.

This entity first made itself known to the Herrmann family of Seaford, New York, in early February 1958. Mrs. Herrmann had just welcomed her children Lucille and Jimmy home from school when several bottles in various rooms of the house all popped their tops and spilled their contents. The family thought that maybe pressure had built up in the bottles. But the tops were all the twist-off kind, so there seemed to be no rational explanation.

After the same thing happened several more times, Mr. Herrmann began to suspect that his son Jimmy was somehow playing a trick on the family. So Mr. Herrmann carefully watched Jimmy while the incidents occurred. He realized that unless his son was a future Houdini, there was no way that the boy could be responsible. With no "ghost busters" to consult, Mr. Herrmann did the next best thing he could in 1958: He called the police.

The police were skeptical at first, but after witnessing some of the episodes themselves, they decided to investigate. They had no answers, and the incidents kept happening. They even had a priest bless the house and sprinkle holy water in each of its rooms, but that didn't help either. They thought about trying an exorcism but decided against it because the incidents didn't seem to be the work of a demon. They seemed to be the antics of a poltergeist.

Explanation Unknown

Word of the events attracted the attention of curiosity seekers and the media. All explanations—from the scientific (sonic booms, strong drafts, freakish magnetic waves) to the weird and wacky (Russian satellite *Sputnik*)—were considered and dismissed. Although this was the Cold War era (a time in U.S. history when tensions were high between the United States and the Soviet Union), it was unclear how tormenting a single American family fit into the Soviets' plan to rule the world.

What was far more worrisome was that the incidents seemed to be getting more violent. Instead of just bottles popping open, objects like a sugar bowl, a record player, and a heavy bookcase were tossed around. Fortunately, help arrived in the form of experts from Duke University. Their theory was that someone in the house was unknowingly moving objects via Recurrent Spontaneous Psychokinesis (RSPK), which means moving objects with the mind. Children seemed to attract such activity, and the Duke team discovered that Jimmy had been at or near the scene of the incidents most of the time.

When one of the researchers spent time with Jimmy—playing cards, helping him with his homework, or just talking—the unusual activity declined. Two more incidents occurred in early March before the Seaford Poltergeist apparently packed its bags and moved on. After 67 recorded incidents in five weeks, the lives of the Herrmann family returned to normal. To this day, it is still unknown exactly what caused the strange events in the Herrmann household in early 1958.

"He's stuck, that's what it is. He's in between worlds. You know it happens sometimes that the spirit gets yanked out so fast that the essence still feels it has work to do here."

—Oda Mae Brown (Whoopi Goldberg's character in *Ghost*)

Spectral Ships and Phantom Crews

Ghost ships seem to have the ability to slip back and forth between this world and the next. They often appear as signs of impending doom. Come with us as we set sail in search of some of the most famous ghost ships in history.

Mary Celeste

On November 7, 1872, the *Mary Celeste* left New York for Genoa, Italy. On board were Captain Benjamin Briggs, his family, and a crew of seven.

On December 4, the crew of the *Dei Gratia* found the *Mary Celeste* abandoned. There was plenty of food and water on the ship, but the only living soul on board was a cat. The crew and the captain's family were missing, and they left no clues about where they went. The last entry in the captain's log was dated almost two weeks prior to the ship's discovery. Somehow the vessel had sailed itself all that time.

What happened to the *Mary Celeste* and those on board remains a mystery. Many believe that a ghostly crew sailed the ship and kept it safe until it was found.

Iron Mountain

A ship disappearing on the high seas is one thing, but on a river? That's exactly what happened to the *Iron Mountain.* In June 1872, the 180-foot-long riverboat left New Orleans on its way to Pittsburgh. The vessel was cruising on the Mississippi

River with a crew of more than 50 men. The *Iron Mountain* stopped at Vicksburg, Mississippi, to pick up additional cargo that was towed behind the steamer on barges. The next day, the *Iron Mountain* vanished. The barges were found, but the *Iron Mountain* and its crew were never seen nor heard from again. For years after it disappeared, riverboat captains whispered about how the *Iron Mountain* was simply sucked into another world through a ghostly gateway.

Palatine

According to legend, shortly after Christmas 1738, the *Princess Augusta* ran aground and broke into pieces on the coast of Block Island, Rhode Island. Nearly 130 years later, poet John Greenleaf Whittier renamed the European vessel and told his version of the shipwreck in his poem *The Palatine.* Today, strange lights are still reported in the waters around Block Island, especially between Christmas and New Year's Day. They are said to be the fiery ghost ship.

Edmund Fitzgerald

When it comes to ghost ships, the *Edmund Fitzgerald* is the biggest. The 720-foot-long freighter moved iron ore across the Great Lakes beginning in the late 1950s. On November 10, 1975, the mammoth ship sank during a violent storm without ever calling for help. All 29 crew members were thought to be dead, but their bodies were never found.

Almost ten years to the day after the *"Fitz"* sank, a strange dark ship was seen on Lake Superior. One look at the monstrous vessel was all that witnesses needed to recognize it as the *Edmund Fitzgerald.*

Flying Dutchman

Stories say that during the 1800s, Captain Hendrick Vanderdecken was attempting to sail the *Flying Dutchman* around the Cape of Good Hope in southern Africa when a violent storm erupted. Rather than pull into port, the stubborn captain claimed that he would navigate around the Cape even if it took him forever to do so. The ship and its crew were lost in the storm, and, as promised by Vanderdecken, they were condemned to sail the high seas for all eternity.

Almost immediately after the ship was lost, people from all over the world began spotting it moving silently through the ocean. It often seemed to be glowing eerily. Because of the legend associated with Captain Vanderdecken, sightings of the *Flying Dutchman* are now thought to be bad omens. Case in point: One of the most recent sightings of the spectral vessel occurred off the coast of North Carolina's Outer Banks just prior to Hurricane Isabel's arrival in 2003.

Haunted eBay

Many people drive hours to reach haunted destinations, but a new trend might save some gas money: bringing the ghost into your own home! All you need is a computer and a PayPal account.

Since the early days of eBay, people have offered all sorts of "haunted" items for sale on the online auction site. Some of the objects have sold for thousands of dollars. The site even offers a Guide to Buying Haunted Items. So what sorts of haunted objects can be found on eBay? Read on to find out.

Haunted Cane

After Mary Anderson's father passed away in 2004, her five-year-old son was convinced that his ghost was haunting the house. Specifically, the boy believed that the spirit had taken up residence in an old cane. To convince her son that the spirit was gone, Anderson put the "haunted" cane up for sale on eBay. A bidding war resulted in 132 bids. When the dust had settled, website GoldenPalace.com shelled out a mind-boggling $65,000 for the haunted cane. This was the most expensive haunted item sold on eBay so far.

Haunted iPhone

In 2008, people lined up for the chance to buy their very own iPhone. Around that same time, someone offered up a haunted iPhone on eBay. Not only did this iPhone act strangely and make odd noises (like laughing out loud), but the ghostly image of what appeared to be Steve Jobs (who was still alive at the time) also seemed to be "burned" onto the iPhone's screen.

With a starting price of more than $8 million, the haunted iPhone seemed unlikely to sell. Several days after it was posted, the auction was taken down without receiving a single bid.

Ghost in a Bottle

"Supernatural or novelty? You decide!" That was the sales pitch for the Ghost in a Bottle when several of the items appeared on eBay in 2008 for $20 each. The seller wouldn't guarantee what would happen if a customer decided to open one of these bottles and release the ghost inside, but that didn't stop people from buying them.

The creator of the "original" Ghost in a Bottle no longer sells them on eBay. Similar items occasionally go up for auction starting at around $29.

Spooky Dolls A-Plenty

By far, the most popular "haunted" items on eBay are dolls. On any given day, hundreds of listings promise to deliver a haunted doll to your door. While most haunted dolls sell for around $25, some go for $100 or more, especially if they're particularly creepy looking.

Antique Hat Pin

The seller of a haunted antique hat pin claimed to be a paranormal researcher with more than 45 years of experience who was downsizing his personal collection. The pin was supposedly found inside a secret room of a haunted mansion. The seller stated that he'd seen a "blue, glowing streak that swirls" around the item. The pin was also known for moving on its own and for "spinning wildly on a table." The auction's sole bidder paid $15 for the pin.

Human Soul

Some people believe that ghosts are the restless souls of the deceased. Perhaps that's why there was so much interest when college student Adam Burtle put his soul up for auction in 2001. Believe it or not, eBay policy dictates that souls fall under the site's "no body parts" policy, so it usually shuts down such auctions. But this one slipped through, possibly because no one was bidding on it. Adam's ex-girlfriend bid $6.66, and it appeared that she might win the auction. But then a bidding war erupted in the final hour of the sale. In the end, the soul sold for $400 to a bidder from Des Moines, Iowa. The winner has yet to try and collect her prize. As for Adam Burtle, eBay suspended his account.

Spirits Live On at the West Virginia Penitentiary

All of West Virginia's executions used to take place at the state penitentiary. That may be one reason why this prison has more than its fair share of ghosts. Torture, violence, murder, and suicide were all common occurrences during its days as a prison. It's no wonder that some of the people who lived there still roam its gloomy, dark halls.

Built in the late 1800s, the West Virginia Penitentiary in Moundsville has the look of a spooky storybook castle. It was originally designed to house 480 inmates, but its population soared from 250 prisoners when it opened in 1876 to 2,400 in the early 1930s. With as many as three men sharing one tiny five-foot-by-seven-foot cell, living conditions there were horrid.

Beaten Spirits

Wardens at the West Virginia Pen issued severe punishments for inmates who misbehaved. Prisoners were tortured, whipped, and beaten. One spirit that lingers there is said to be that of Robert, an inmate who was beaten to death.

Over the years, many deaths occurred within the prison's walls. Some were brought on by violent treatment, poor living conditions, and illness. In addition, a total of 94 men were executed there, 85 by hanging and 9 by the electric chair. One execution began with a mishap when a man who had been sentenced to hang fell through the floor before the noose could be tied around his neck. He had to be picked up and taken back upstairs, where he was then hung successfully. It is said that his spirit still wanders around the area where he died.

As early as the 1930s, folks at the prison began seeing ghosts and getting eerie feelings that an invisible entity was standing close by. One specter that is often seen is that of a maintenance man who spied on the inmates and liked to get them into trouble. He met his end when a group of prisoners attacked him in a bathroom, which is where his earthbound spirit remains today.

Ghostly activity also takes place in the shower area, in the chapel, along death row, and at the execution site. And don't forget the front gate where the turnstiles move by themselves—perhaps admitting a "new" batch of inmates.

One particularly frightening spirit at the West Virginia Pen is that of the "shadow man." His misty shape has been spotted lurking in the dark, giving off a bone-chilling feeling to those who see him. In fact, many of the spirits there are intimidating. They often leave people with a sense that they are being watched or even followed.

Unruly Spirits

One area of the prison that investigators have found to be swarming with paranormal activity is "the Sugar Shack"—an area where inmates went to exercise. There is no official record of a death occurring there, but many people have felt cold spots and heard unexplained noises, such as screams and arguing voices. Some visitors have even felt unseen hands poking them in the back or stroking them on the cheek.

If you like ghosts or history—or both—the West Virginia Pen is well worth the trip. But beware of this group of spirits. They were unhappy in life and are still unhappy in death. So if you feel the touch of something that you can't see, it might be a good idea to run!

Chasing Ghosts on the Small Screen

Firsthand encounters with ghosts and true tales of hauntings have never been more popular among television viewers.

Unsolved Mysteries

Unsolved Mysteries scours the globe looking for supposedly true stories of the unexplained. The show attempts to reenact real-life mysteries using eyewitness accounts. Of course, many such events involve ghosts, poltergeists, and other paranormal phenomena, so it's not surprising that many viewers are left believing that our spirits live on after we die.

Ghost Hunters

When it premiered in 2004, *Ghost Hunters* was one of the first reality TV shows to chronicle the activities of real-life paranormal investigators—in this case Jason Hawes and Grant Wilson. Jason and Grant are plumbers by trade, but together they created The Atlantic Paranormal Society (TAPS). Jason and Grant both had ghostly encounters before starting TAPS, but they prefer not to discuss those incidents. Unlike some of the other ghost-hunting shows on television, the TAPS team members try to find reasonable explanations for the phenomena that they investigate. Even so, they have experienced their share of activities that they simply can't explain, including shadow figures, strange noises, and objects that have moved on their own.

Paranormal State

While attending Penn State University in 2001, Ryan Buell started the Paranormal Research Society (PRS). By 2006, what began as a student club had gained national attention. Soon, camera crews were following PRS members on their quest to investigate claims of ghosts, demons, and poltergeists. The result was *Paranormal State.*

The majority of ghost-hunting TV shows investigate at well-known haunted locations across the United States. But *Paranormal State* focuses more on helping average Americans deal with the unseen (and often unwelcome) visitors in their homes. Sometimes this can be risky for the PRS team. Ryan claims that during one investigation, he was threatened by a demon that stalked him for years afterward.

Ghost Adventures

Since 2008, professional ghost hunters Nick Groff, Aaron Goodwin, and the sometimes over-the-top Zak Bagans have been exploring some of the most haunted places in the world. At the beginning of each investigation, the team obtains background information about the location and the alleged haunting. Then they set up video cameras in areas where the most activity has been reported. Finally, they are locked inside the building overnight while they conduct their investigation. Bagans has been known to provoke evil spirits using aggressive language and trigger objects, including his own tattoos. During an investigation at Bobby Mackey's Music World in Wilder, Kentucky, Bagans was scratched by what he believes was a demonic entity.

Psychic Kids

Many people mock Haley Joel Osment's famous line from *The Sixth Sense* ("I see dead people"). But there are many highly sensitive children in the world who really do see spirits and have the ability to communicate with them. Since 2008, the show *Psychic Kids* has introduced viewers to some of these youngsters as they (and their families) come to terms with their special gifts. Noted psychic/medium Chip Coffey and psychotherapist Edy Nathan coach the "Children of the Paranormal" so that they can better deal with the spirits they see, put their fears to rest, and be proud of their unique abilities.

Celebrity Ghost Stories

No, it's not about the ghosts of famous people. This series' title refers to celebrities who describe their supposedly true encounters with the supernatural. Since the show's debut in 2009, stars such as Miley Cyrus, William Baldwin, Regis Philbin, and Haylie Duff have all shared their terrifying tales on the show. In a 2010 episode, Tracy Nelson (the daughter of 1950s teen idol Ricky Nelson) recalled some of the paranormal phenomena that she experienced growing up in a home that was haunted by the ghost of actor and ladies' man Errol Flynn. She also shared her belief that a dark force in the house brought about her father's tragic and untimely death in a plane crash in 1985.

Ghost Lab

In 1990, while visiting Gettysburg, Pennsylvania, Brad Klinge witnessed (and videotaped) a group of ghostly soldiers at the historic battlefield. In 2007, Brad and his brother Barry formed Everyday Paranormal, a group that specializes in using science "to prove the existence of the paranormal." From 2009 to 2011, the Klinge brothers crisscrossed the country examining some of the most haunted locations in America on *Ghost Lab.* The Everyday Paranormal team consulted with scientific experts from highly respected universities. Their goal was to present the facts and let the viewers decide whether or not they believed that something paranormal had occurred.

My Ghost Story

My Ghost Story first hit the television airwaves in 2010. On the show, eyewitnesses discuss their encounters with the spirit world. The incidents are reenacted and accompanied by personal photos, security-camera footage, and home videos. In one particularly disturbing episode, a couple shared the horrifying experiences they had while living in a home where a family was brutally killed by an ax murderer. The troubled spirit of a neighbor who may have witnessed the gruesome act haunts the house next door.

Married to the Mob . . . Even in Death

When people hear the phrase "mob haunts," they probably think of places where members of the Mafia or other gangs hang out. But the following locations are literally haunted by their connections to organized crime. Whether they are trying to warn the living of the consequences of their actions or committing acts of revenge, these restless spirits want to make sure that no one ever forgets what happens when you tangle with the mob.

Never Leaving Las Vegas

The ghost of Benjamin "Bugsy" Siegel is a very active spirit. That's not surprising considering that he was one of the most famous mobsters in history. By the time he was a teenager, Brooklyn-born Siegel had started a gang with friend Meyer Lansky on New York's Lower East Side. In the 1920s, Siegel's activities in gambling, selling illegal alcohol, and stealing cars caught the attention of the New York underworld. He was sent to California to watch over the mob's gambling operations and to arrange the murders of its enemies, which he often carried out himself. He also became obsessed with Las Vegas, Nevada.

Siegel's dream—which he convinced the mob to pay for—was to turn this tiny town in the desert into the most glamorous gambling destination in the United States. This dream became a reality in December 1946, when he opened the Flamingo casino and hotel. The Flamingo got off to a slow start, so mob bosses demanded that Siegel turn business around—or else. By 1947, he believed that the operation had become successful, but what he didn't know was that the bosses had already condemned him to death. On June 20, 1947, Siegel was killed in a hail of gunfire at the home of his girlfriend, Virginia Hill.

Siegel died instantly, but his spirit never really left the scene of the crime. Since then, witnesses have watched in awe as a ghostly male figure suddenly appears, runs across the mansion's living room, ducks for cover, and then disappears. A psychic confirmed that the man was none other than Bugsy Siegel, who seems to be doomed to spend eternity trying to hide from his killers.

Bugsy Siegel's spirit has also been seen hanging out by the pool table and in the two bathrooms of the Flamingo's Presidential Suite (which was his home in life). Guests have reported moving cold spots and objects in the suite that inexplicably changed locations or disappeared entirely.

Even after the Flamingo was demolished in 1993, Siegel's ghost remained. He's been observed in the new hotel's wedding chapel and in the rose garden near a monument dedicated to him. It seems appropriate that the spirit of a man who took so many lives must prowl his old stomping grounds for all eternity.

Dark Spirits Torment La Palazza

Given that the mob essentially built Las Vegas, it is not surprising that many gangster ghosts call the town their eternal home. Some of Sin City's darkest spirits like to hang out at a mansion known as "La Palazza." For years, there were rumors that the house contained a room that was used just for murders. A former owner even found guns hidden under the floorboards there.

Previous residents experienced many disturbing incidents while living in the house. A former owner's dog would shake and follow an invisible being with its eyes. This man later saw what had disturbed his dog so much. It was a spectral older woman wearing a wide-brimmed hat and large sunglasses.

The same man and his girlfriend once watched as wine-glasses moved by themselves and then crashed down onto the tabletop. The girlfriend also claimed that disembodied male voices repeatedly made rude comments about her, especially while she showered. In addition, she heard voices coming from the attic and saw the ghostly figure of a tall man. When a medium asked this spirit what his business was, he replied that he "did whatever needed to be done" when he was alive.

The spirits of the house seemed to negatively affect its male residents. One man had the sensation that unseen hands were choking him. He also felt that the home's dark energy was possessing him. After finding bloodstains in what might have been the room that was used for executions, he became overwhelmed with rage and began carrying a gun. He decided to sell the house before it caused him to do something that would ruin his life.

In 2010, the team from the TV show *Ghost Adventures* went to the mansion to investigate. Interviews with the former homeowners left the team members so concerned that they were dealing with a demonic entity that they brought a crucifix and holy water with them when they were locked inside the house overnight. While they were there, fully charged batteries were instantly drained, cameras blacked out when ghosts were asked to show themselves, and the readings on the team's EMF detector spiked. And just as one of the previous owners had experienced, the physical features and personality of investigator Zak Bagans seemed to change throughout the session. The team concluded that the place is full of dark energy, perhaps due to the unspeakable acts committed at the site and the spirits of those who remain.

Is That Really John Dillinger?

Phantom mobsters also spook the city of Chicago. The ghost of another famous gangster is said to roam an alley near the Biograph Theater on the city's north side. On July 22, 1934, notorious bank robber and Public Enemy No. 1 John Dillinger was shot and killed by FBI agents after watching a movie at the Biograph. His death was widely reported in the media, but some said that the corpse was not Dillinger. They thought it was a low-level gangster who had been set up to impersonate him.

Regardless of who died there, people have since observed the hazy figure of a man fleeing, only to fall and then disappear. Others have reported feeling cold spots and inexplicable chilly breezes.

No Escape from Their Actions

Some mobsters inflicted violent deaths upon their enemies and some met brutal ends themselves. Others were caught by the law and imprisoned for their crimes. And a fortunate few lived long lives, during which they were never held accountable for their dastardly deeds. Wherever they are, in life or death, mobsters and gangsters leave their marks. No matter how they finished out their lives on earth, it seems that some members of the mob remain eternally ruthless.

Remember the Alamo!

No one knows for sure why ghosts choose certain places to haunt. One explanation suggests that many earthbound spirits are victims of tragedy. One of the greatest tragedies in U.S. history occurred when General Santa Anna's Mexican army slaughtered nearly 200 Texans during the Battle of the Alamo. The tales of those gallant men who refused to give up the mission-turned-fortress remain with us today. In fact, it seems as though many of those brave souls haven't left.

Standing Their Ground

In the mid-1830s, the land we now call Texas was owned by Mexico. In October 1835, war broke out between the Mexican army and settlers in Texas. The Texans wanted to gain their independence from Mexico. By early February 1836, the young government of Texas was a mess, and additional troops for the army were in short supply. So when Colonel James Bowie, Colonel William Travis, and Davy

Crockett arrived in San Antonio, they knew that little help was on the way. The weakened group of around 180 soldiers prepared to face a Mexican army of more than 1,800.

General Santa Anna and his troops attacked the Alamo from a distance for 12 days before charging forward on March 6. The brave soldiers inside the fort fought valiantly, killing or wounding hundreds of Mexican soldiers in the process. But the Texans were hopelessly outnumbered, and the battle was over in less than 90 minutes. Only a handful of the fighting Texans survived, along with the women and children whom Santa Anna spared from the slaughter. (The soldiers who did survive were later executed.)

Protective Phantoms

Several weeks after the fateful battle took place, Santa Anna ordered his men to destroy the Alamo. He wanted to erase any evidence of the Texans' brave stand. The task fell to Colonel Sanchez, who rode with his men to tear down the old church. But as they prepared to do so, six phantom monks appeared from the walls of the Alamo. Armed with flaming swords, the monks made their demands clear. "Do not touch the walls of the Alamo!" the spirits shrieked. Frightened for their lives and their very souls, Colonel Sanchez and his men retreated to camp to report to General Andrade.

The general was not impressed by the story. He brought a group of soldiers and a cannon back to the mission to finish the job himself. Just as he ordered his troops to aim the cannon at the chapel door, the monks appeared again. Armed with their flaming swords and screaming their demands, they scared the troops and spooked their horses. General Andrade was thrown from his steed, and when he got back on, he turned his attention back to the Alamo. It was then that a wall of fire appeared to erupt from the ground, preventing him from getting any closer to the mission. To his further horror, the thick black smoke from the fire quickly took the form of a large man with a ball of fire in each of his spectral hands. The general ran and never returned. But this was only the beginning of the Alamo's supernatural history.

Guarding Ghosts

In the years after the Battle of the Alamo, the fort was used as a jail. During this time, newspapers reported sightings of a guard patrolling the roof. The guard was spotted walking east to west and back again each night. However, the authorities claimed that they'd never stationed a man there. In fact, anyone who bothered to watch the guard for more than a moment noticed that he quickly vanished. Most guards and officers refused to patrol the building at night because they kept hearing horrible moans in the darkness. It sounded like Mexican soldiers were stabbing a soldier to death. It was as if a soldier's final moments were being reenacted over and over again each night. The men also reported feeling as though eyes were following them throughout the building. This ominous presence seems to stalk visitors to the Alamo to this day.

Wandering Wraiths

The spirits guarding the Alamo aren't the only specters that make themselves known at the site. Visitors often report seeing a young blond-haired boy in a window over what is now a gift shop.

It is also said that every year in early March, around the anniversary of the massacre, a horse can be heard galloping on the pavement at dawn. Some believe that it's a spectral messenger who is still trying to reach Colonel Travis.

Soldier Anthony Wolfe and his young sons also died at the hands of the Mexican army during the Battle of the Alamo. The ghostly boys are said to go along on the daily tours of the mission. Many tour groups have reported seeing the two young boys following them. But when the group reaches the chapel, the boys vanish. Park rangers have also spotted a man dressed in period clothing. When they follow him across the grounds, he fades from view when he reaches the chapel.

Celebrity Specters

Not all the ghosts at the Alamo are unknown figures. One spirit that is often seen on the grounds wears a buckskin shirt, moccasins, and a coonskin cap. Sometimes he stands at attention with a rifle at his side. Other times he's leaning on a wall near the chapel, dying from his wounds. One ranger even claimed that he got close enough to determine that it was definitely Davy Crockett and that he watched as phantom soldiers in Mexican uniforms attacked the famed frontiersman. Multiple people have observed Davy Crockett from different vantage points at the same time.

Finally, there's the case of actor John Wayne, who became obsessed with the old mission while he was directing his epic western *The Alamo* (1960) on location. Since his death in 1979, John Wayne's ghost has been spotted at the Alamo on more than one occasion. He usually just wanders the grounds, but occasionally he is seen talking to other restless spirits. If John Wayne did indeed choose to haunt the Alamo, he certainly has plenty of company.

RIP RIP RIP RIP

The Cashtown Inn

Located near Gettysburg, Pennsylvania's historic battlefield, the Cashtown Inn is considered one of the region's hot spots for paranormal activity. That's no small feat in an area well known for its otherworldly inhabitants.

The Setting

The Battle of Gettysburg is perhaps the most famous of all Civil War conflicts. This hard-fought confrontation—which was waged from July 1 to July 3, 1863—served as a turning point in the war that divided the nation. Union troops earned a momentous victory, but it came at a cost: The battle resulted in nearly 51,000 total casualties, including almost 8,000 deaths.

Gettysburg has become "Civil War central" to historians and tourists. Not surprisingly, paranormal activity is off the charts in these parts, so much so that many area residents make a living offering ghost tours, ghostly Gettysburg souvenirs, and the like. And fans of the supernatural regard the Cashtown Inn as one of Gettysburg's most haunted hotels. With much of the building's history stained by the bloody battle, this comes as no surprise.

Three Days of Hell

The town of Cashtown served as a Confederate base of operations before and during the Battle of Gettysburg. Soon after the blue and the gray traded fire, wounded Confederate soldiers were brought to the Cashtown Inn's basement, which had been turned into an operating room. So many surgeries were performed there that a nearby stream allegedly turned red with blood. Small mountains of severed body parts were scattered around the inn, and screams and moans filled the premises. By July 4, the outlook at the camp was grim. Realizing that they had suffered a major defeat, the Confederates knew that it was time to collect themselves, physically and mentally, and retreat to Virginia.

Stirrings

After the battle, the Cashtown Inn returned to serving guests. It remained successful through 1948, when a new highway took traffic (and tourists) away from the hotel. Over the next few decades, the inn's condition worsened. Finally, in 1987, the building underwent a major restoration. That's when the tales of supernatural sightings began to come as quickly as gunfire. From ghostly shadows of men dressed in Confederate uniforms to the sound of phantom footsteps, the Cashtown Inn experienced paranormal activity in every one of its rooms.

Ghosts and Other Practical Jokers

In a lighthearted variation of the old "knock, knock" prank, playful poltergeists have been known to tap loudly on the door of Room 4. But when occupants answer the door, no one is there.

Sounds of men on horseback once woke a guest in Room 4. When he checked to see what was causing the commotion, nothing was found. But the noises continued. In the morning, the annoyed guest complained to the owner. When the man returned to his room, his suitcases were fully packed. This prompted him to ask if it was normal for the staff to pack guests' bags. The innkeeper assured the man that none of his employees backed his bags.

Of course, not all of the ghosts at the Cashtown Inn are this helpful. Sullen spirits that are dressed in full Confederate uniform have been seen lingering around the inn. They tend to frighten guests, but they are simply part of the scenery to employees.

Proof or Consequences

The Atlantic Paranormal Society (aka TAPS)—the stars of television's *Ghost Hunters*—put the Cashtown Inn to the test in 2008. During their four days of investigation, they recorded the sound of boot-clad footsteps coming from the unoccupied floor above them. They also filmed a picture frame moving across a table by itself. This can mean only one thing: The ghosts of the Cashtown Inn are still up to their old tricks.

Was *The Exorcist* Really Based on a True Story?

In the 1973 film The Exorcist, *Linda Blair plays a young girl who is possessed by a demon. The story was based on a best-selling novel by William Peter Blatty. Naturally, everyone wants to know if the story is true. The answer to that question is... maybe.*

In January 1949, a 13-year-old boy named Roland and his family lived in Mount Rainier, Maryland. That's when they began to hear scratching sounds coming from behind the walls and inside the ceiling of their house. Believing that their home was infested with mice, Roland's parents called an exterminator. But the exterminator found no evidence of rodents in the house. After that, the family started to hear unexplained footsteps in the home, and objects such as dishes and furniture seemed to relocate on their own.

But these incidents would seem minor compared to what came next. Roland claimed that an invisible entity attacked him. He also said that his bed shook so violently that he couldn't sleep. The sheets and blankets were repeatedly ripped from his bed and tossed onto the floor. One time, Roland tried to grab them, but he was yanked onto the floor with the bedcovers still clenched in his fists.

Roland's aunt Tillie had a strong interest in the spirit world, and she had taught him how to use a Ouija board before she died. Some blamed the Ouija board for causing the trouble, saying that it had invited a demon into the home.

Not Such Good Vibrations

By this time, the family was convinced that an evil entity was causing the strange events in their home. They decided to ask a minister named Reverend Schulze for help. Reverend Schulze prayed for Roland and had his congregation do so as well. He even took Roland to his own home so the boy could get some sleep. But both the bed and an armchair that Roland tried to sleep in there vibrated and moved, so he still couldn't rest. Reverend Schulze noticed that Roland

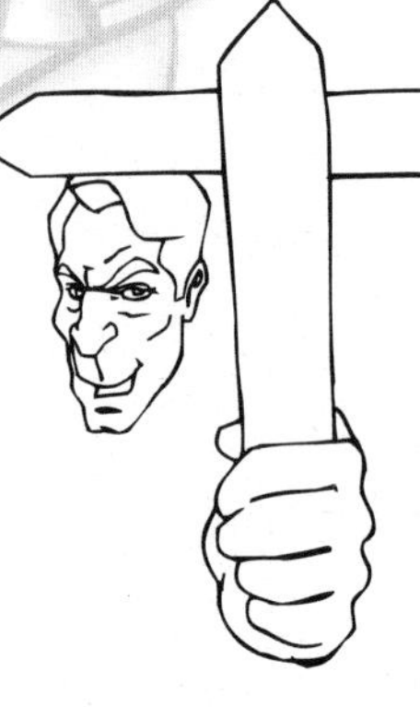

seemed to be in a trance while these incidents occurred.

If Reverend Schulze had any doubt that it was time to call for backup, he was certainly convinced when red scratches mysteriously appeared on Roland's body. These marks were then replaced by words that looked like they were made by claws. The word *Louis* was clearly visible, which was interpreted as St. Louis, Roland's mother's hometown. With all signs pointing to the need for an exorcism (a religious practice used to get rid of an evil spirit or demon), Father Edward Albert Hughes of St. James Catholic Church was called.

Truth or Fiction?

Father Hughes went to see Roland and was upset when the boy spoke to him in Latin—a language that was unknown to the youth. Father Hughes decided to perform an exorcism. The priest was supposedly so shaken by the ordeal that he was never the same again.

During Roland's visit with Father Hughes, the priest suggested using blessed candles and special prayers to help the boy. But when Roland's mother did this, a comb flew across the room. It hit the candles and blew them out. Other objects also flew around the room, and at one point, a Bible was thrown at the boy's feet.

An attempt was made to baptize Roland into the Catholic faith as a way of helping him, but this didn't work out so well. As his uncle drove him to the church, the boy grabbed him by the throat and screamed that the baptism wouldn't work.

The Battle of St. Louis

The family members were at their wits' end, so they decided to stay with relatives in the St. Louis area. Unfortunately, the distance between Maryland and Missouri was no big deal to the invisible entity, and the assaults on Roland continued. In St. Louis, a relative introduced the boy and his family to Jesuit priest Father William Bowdern. Father Bowdern teamed up with another priest named Father Raymond J. Bishop in an effort to help the family.

Several times, Father Bishop tried to stop the attacks on Roland, but nothing worked. After he sprinkled the boy's mattress with holy water in the shape of a cross, the attacks stopped. But when Father Bishop left the room, Roland suddenly screamed in pain. When his pajama top was pulled up, Roland had numerous scratches across his belly. He was in the presence of several witnesses at all times, so he could not have scratched himself.

After more nights of violence against Roland, Father Bishop returned—this time with Father Bowdern. They prayed in the boy's room and then left. But as soon as they did, loud noises started coming from the room. When family members investigated, they found that an extremely heavy bookcase had turned around, a bench had flipped upside down, and the boy's mattress was once again shaking. At this point, it was decided that another exorcism was the only solution.

The exorcism was a desperate battle that was carried out over the course of several months. Some of it took place at the church, some of it at a hospital, and some of it at Roland's home. One source says that the boy was exorcised no less than 20 times. During this time, practically everything and anything typically associated with an exorcism occurred. Roland's body jerked in uncontrollable spasms, he spewed projectile vomit, and he spit and cursed at the priests. He also mentioned information that he couldn't possibly have known. (However, his head didn't spin completely around like Linda Blair's did in *The Exorcist.*)

Gone, but Certainly Not Forgotten

Eventually, Father Bowdern's persistence paid off. He repeatedly practiced the exorcism ritual on Roland. While he was doing so, he had to ignore the physical and verbal abuse hurled at him by the entity that had taken control of Roland's body. Finally, in mid-April 1949, Roland spoke with a voice that identified itself as St. Michael. He ordered Satan and all demons to leave the boy alone. For the next few minutes, Roland went into a tremendous rage. It was as if good and evil were battling inside of him. Suddenly, he became quiet, turned to the priests, and simply said, "He's gone."

The entity *was* gone, and fortunately, Roland remembered little about the ordeal. Some months later, a 20-year-old college student named William Peter Blatty spotted an article in *The Washington Post* about Roland's experience. He let the idea of demonic possession kick around in his brain for years before finally writing his book, which became a best seller. Out of privacy concerns, Blatty changed so many details from the actual case that the source was virtually unrecognizable—until the intense publicity surrounding the movie forced the "real" story out.

Over the years, there have been numerous theories suggested about the incident. Some say that it was an elaborate hoax gone too far. Others claim that it was the result of demonic possession or poltergeist activity. Regardless, this case continues to be a part of American culture.

"There are an infinite number of universes existing side by side and through which our consciousnesses constantly pass. In these universes, all possibilities exist. You are alive in some, long dead in others, and never existed in still others. Many of our 'ghosts' could indeed be visions of people going about their business in a parallel universe or another time—or both."

—Paul F. Eno, *Faces at the Window*

Pets That Have Passed . . . and Returned

Many of us have had pets that will live on forever in our hearts. Some people keep their pets' ashes. A few go so far as to have their former companions stuffed. But is there any other way to keep them around? Some pet owners have found that their furry friends continue to linger around the house after they pass away . . . just in a slightly less furry, more spectral form.

Shep the Dog

Is it love that brings back a beloved pet? It was probably a factor in the case of Joe and his beloved dog Shep. One night, Joe was walking home after returning from serving in World War II. His dog Shep met him along the way. As Joe was about to cross a bridge, Shep began to bark and pull on his master's pant leg. The dog wouldn't stop, so finally, Joe gave in and took a different route home. When Joe arrived at home, he told his family that Shep made him go another way. Everyone looked at him strangely, and then Joe's father told him that Shep had died the previous winter. Joe also learned that the middle section of the bridge he was going to take had been washed away by heavy rains. So the spectral Shep saved Joe's life.

Big Black Dog

When Harry Potter sees a big black dog, he's comforted to know that it's his godfather Sirius. But when most of us see a similar apparition, it's a bit scary. Children are more likely to

see spirits. That was the case with a person who reported seeing a ghostly black dog as a child. One night, the child woke up to find a large black dog sitting in the doorway of the bedroom. The dog looked like a Doberman, with short ears and short hair, but it appeared as a shadow with no face. When the child screamed, the dog simply vanished. The same thing happened a few nights later. That time, the dog disappeared when a light was turned on. The dog was not a pet, and it was never seen again.

A Spectral Black Cat

Home renovations can uncover treasures from the past. That's what happened to a family when they built a loft in the old house that had once belonged to the wife's mother. One night, the wife saw a skinny black cat walking down the stairs. Although the family did have a cat at the time, it was an orange tabby that was about ten pounds heavier than the feline she saw. The woman forgot all about the cat until her daughter said that she wouldn't play in the loft anymore because she didn't like seeing the black ghost-cat run by. No one else ever saw the phantom feline. But an old photo of the wife's mother as a young girl showed her posing in the backyard holding a small black cat in her arms.

Houdini the Terrier

Famous magician Harry Houdini promised his wife that if he could visit her from the Other Side, he would. It seems that Houdini wasn't able to pull off that stunt. But a pet terrier (that was named for the illusionist) did. When the 13-year-old dog died suddenly, his family was understandably grief-stricken. One night, the woman heard the dog's footsteps following her down the hallway, just like he did in life. Her daughter also heard the footsteps and heard scratching too. But no one actually saw the phantom pooch. Houdini's ghostly visits comforted the woman and her family. But they decided that they should let him move on. The woman told Houdini that she loved him but that he should cross over into Heaven. They haven't heard the dog since then, but they believe that they'll be reunited with him one day.

Kemway

Sonja was in Kenya with the Peace Corps when she had an unusual experience with her dog Kemway. One day, she left to help a friend, so she locked her two dogs in an outdoor pen. But she realized that she had forgotten something, so she headed back home. On the way, her car had a flat tire. When she got out of the vehicle, she found herself staring into the eyes of a rabid hyena. Then she heard Kemway growl behind her. The dog and the hyena fought each other viciously. Sonja realized that neither animal would make it out alive, so she drove home to get her shotgun. When she got there, her neighbor ran outside, apologizing and begging for her forgiveness. He had been driving down the road when he accidentally hit Kemway, who died instantly. He showed Sonja the dog's body by the road. It seems that Kemway's ghost appeared from out of nowhere to save his beloved owner.

Cindy the Dog

Some pets return to haunt people other than their masters. That was the case with Bon and Cindy, the neighbor dog. Cindy's family was often away, so she would play with Bon and her dogs. Cindy especially liked to come over when a storm was coming. One day after Cindy passed away, Bon heard a familiar scratching at the front door when a storm was brewing. Bon opened the door, half-expecting to find Cindy, but there was nothing there. The family still hears Cindy scratching at the door whenever a storm rolls in.

Cheddar the Cat

A woman found a stray kitten by the side of the road. She took it home to meet her other cat, Biscuit. But Biscuit didn't like the new cat, which the woman named Cheddar. Biscuit hissed at Cheddar and hid in a corner whenever she was around. After a few months, the woman took a photo of the two cats. Soon after, Cheddar meowed to go out—she never returned. When the woman had the photos developed, Biscuit was there, but there was absolutely no sign of Cheddar.

Slave Spirits Still Seek Freedom on the Underground Railroad

In the early 1800s, some kind landowners tried to help people escaping slavery in the South. The route that the slaves took to find freedom in the North was known as the Underground Railroad. This was not an actual train. It was a series of tunnels and hidden rooms where escaped slaves were able to hide for a day or two, get a good meal, and travel onward toward freedom. Their journeys were filled with fear, stress, and sometimes illness or injury. If caught, the slaves were returned to their owners and were punished severely; some were killed on the spot. It's not surprising that slaves who didn't succeed in their quest for freedom still haunt many places along the Underground Railroad.

Deadman's Hill (Willmar, Minnesota)

Minnesota is much farther north of areas that are typically associated with slavery. But for many of the escaped slaves of the mid-1800s, the state was a stop on the way to Canada. Slave ownership was illegal in Minnesota. But unfortunately, it *was* legal at the time for slave traders and bounty hunters to catch escaped slaves anywhere in the country and return them to their "owners." That was the case of one slave who was captured by a bounty hunter and chained to a fence post. The clever slave managed to escape by pulling the post out of the ground. A fence post makes for some pretty heavy luggage, however, and the bounty hunter caught up with the slave again. The two men fought, and the slave killed his captor with the man's own sword. But the slave was also seriously injured in the fight. His body was later found on a farmer's doorstep surrounded by a pool of blood and the uprooted fence post. Both men were buried on the property. The bounty hunter rests atop Deadman's Hill, and the slave is buried next to the farmhouse. The runaway slave's ghost has never been seen, but plenty of people have heard his moans, the rattle of chains, and the distinct sound of something heavy being dragged.

Hannah House (Indianapolis, Indiana)

It was indeed a sad situation when slaves who tried to escape to better lives died in the process. That's what happened at Hannah House, a well-known stop on the Underground Railroad. Slaves waiting in the cellar of the mansion were taken by surprise when someone accidentally tipped over a lantern. Flames surrounded them and trapped them in the basement. They all died within a few minutes.

Since then, visitors have heard voices, moans, and the rattling of chains coming from both the basement and the attic. People have also smelled burning bodies, which has burdened Hannah House with the unpleasant nickname "the house that reeks of death." While no full-bodied apparitions have been spotted there, plenty of unexplained things have happened. Doors open and close by themselves, people report feeling cold breezes even when the windows are closed, and objects move to new locations with no human assistance.

In 2006 and 2007, Indy Ghost Hunters—a local paranormal investigation team—visited Hannah House and recorded numerous EVPs (electronic voice phenomena), including mysterious voices begging for help and warning them to "Get out!" Cameras also captured a shadow moving across the attic, even though all living beings were well out of their range.

Hanson Home (Alton, Illinois)

In 1857, Nathaniel Hanson built a home on a bluff just above the Mississippi River. Inside the house, he created underground rooms and tunnels to help slaves reach freedom. Unfortunately, many slaves lost their lives on this journey, and some spirits may have remained at the Hanson Home.

The structure is now used as an apartment building, and many residents have had their belongings—keys, books, jewelry, and even a bottle of wine—disappear. They almost always reappear a day or so later in an entirely different spot. Like most ghosts, these spirits like to open and close doors and turn the lights on and off. People often report hearing footsteps when no one else is around. Much of this activity seems to take place on the building's upper floors, but the basement has its own set of ghosts—the spirits of slaves who cry out in despair.

Wedgwood Inn (New Hope, Pennsylvania)

If you're a 12-year-old girl, you may be in luck if you're in this small Pennsylvania town hoping to meet a ghost. On her way to freedom in the mid-1800s, a 12-year-old slave girl named Sara stayed at the house that is now the Wedgwood Inn. No one knows the cause of her death, but the building's owners uncovered her remains while renovating the place in 2000. Sara's spirit seems to have stayed at the hotel in order to tell her story to other girls her age. Many young girls have reported meeting her at the inn. When they discuss the details of her life as a slave and how she escaped by using the Underground Railroad, their stories are eerily similar.

Prospect Place (Trinway, Ohio)

A prime stop for slaves heading to Canada, the basement of Prospect Place served hundreds of escapees. Built in 1856, the mansion has 29 rooms, not counting the secret ones located below ground. Today, both slaves and the generous souls who lived on the property are said to haunt the house.

One story about the ghosts of Prospect Place centers on a girl who fell to her death from an upstairs balcony one winter during the early 1860s. Her body was kept in the basement until she could be buried in the spring. The girl's ghost has been seen on the balcony and in the old servants' quarters. She has also been seen and heard crying in the basement. The girl's mother died of an illness soon after the girl's death, and her spirit roams the house as well.

Another slave who died at the house has been seen standing in the basement, as if guarding the girl's body. Also, a spectral husband and wife who were separated while escaping seem to search various areas of the property trying to find each other. And in true poetic justice, in the barn, farmhands hung a bounty hunter who searched for escaped slaves. His ghost still haunts the place where he met his death.

Hickory Hill (Equality, Illinois)

Hickory Hill—which is also known as "The Old Slave House"—is one of the most haunted places in the state of Illinois. Its first owner, John Hart Crenshaw, earned a fortune by operating what is known as a "reverse underground station." Slave catchers and bounty hunters captured escaped slaves and took them to Hickory Hill. From there, Crenshaw sold them back into slavery or put them to work in his salt mines. Visitors to this place have felt cold drafts and the soft brushes of spirits passing by. They've also heard crying and moaning mixed with the rattling of chains.

Riverview Farm (Drexel Hills, Pennsylvania)

The land on which Arlington Cemetery stands today was once part of Riverview Farm, the home of Thomas Garrett Jr. He reportedly helped as many as 2,700 slaves on the road to freedom. While no specific incident would have caused spirits to remain there, evidence suggests that they did. When taking pictures at a nearby home, a photographer captured the aura of something ghostly hovering in the background of an image. Perhaps it's the spirit of one of these brave men and women who were searching for a better life?

School Spirits

When a death occurs at a college or university, it scars students emotionally. It can also leave a ghostly imprint on the building where it occurred. So it's not surprising that institutions of higher learning are among the most haunted places in America.

Hamline University (St. Paul, Minnesota)

About 4,900 students—and several ghosts—attend Hamline University, a liberal arts college in St. Paul, Minnesota. In Old Main—the school's oldest building—a janitor reported seeing a disembodied head with a noose around its neck float past him. Two dormitories on campus also have paranormal connections. On the third floor of Manor Hall, a resident ghost likes to play tricks. There, lamps, fans, and TVs mysteriously turn themselves on and off. And then there's Drew Hall, where an elevator door closed on a student's hand in the 1960s. The young man survived but lost his hand. The phantom hand is said to wander the dorm in search of its body. This story may sound absurd, but try telling that to the numerous students who have reported feeling "icy fingers" touch them during the night.

Nebraska Wesleyan University (Lincoln, Nebraska)

In 1912, Clarissa Mills was chosen to head up the music department and teach piano at Nebraska Wesleyan University. She was well liked by students and her peers. But in 1940, she died at her desk in the C. C. White building. All was normal for the next 20 years, but in 1963, faculty member Coleen Buterbaugh stepped into Clarissa's old office and was never the same again. First she smelled the odor of gas, and then she felt an unknown presence in the room. In front of her stood the ghostly image of a tall, frail woman. It was Clarissa Mills. But that wasn't all. When she looked out the window, everything modern was gone. There were no paved streets, and a recently built sorority house was simply no longer there. Clarissa continued to haunt the building until it burned down in 1973. Buterbaugh, however, quit her job and moved to Colorado.

Henderson State University (Arkadelphia, Arkansas)

The ghost of Henderson State University is said to be the victim of a sad lover's tale. Around 1920, a young woman attended Ouachita Baptist University. Her boyfriend was a student at Arkadelphia College (which is now Henderson State), the Methodist college across the street. They were in love . . . or at least *she* thought so. But the young man decided that the differences between their religions and schools were too much to overcome. When he invited another girl to the Homecoming Dance, the Ouachita student killed herself in despair. Now, each year during Homecoming Week, she is seen drifting through the women's dorms at Henderson, perhaps searching for the young lady who stole her man's heart.

Illinois State University (Normal, Illinois)

Just like in *Ghostbusters* (1984), books in a storage area of Williams Hall at Illinois State University used to fall off shelves and mysteriously rearrange themselves into tall stacks. Students there also reported feeling icy chills. Some even saw a misty entity drifting through the aisles of books. Most believe it was the spirit of Angie Milner, the school's first librarian, who died in 1928. When the books were moved to a new location, the paranormal activity stopped.

Olivet College (Olivet, Michigan)

Olivet College—and the surrounding village of Olivet—hosts a ghost (or ghosts) with a sense of humor. Specters have been seen and photographed passing through walls and peering out of windows. Faint music is heard, but every time someone searches for its source, the music stops. And both students and town residents have often come home to find their possessions mysteriously moved or hidden. Although these incidents have occurred for more than a century and a half, no one seems to know why they started or who these prankster poltergeists might have been in life.

The Original Ghost-Hunting Kit

Many people consider Harry Price to be the first ghost hunter. He is also credited with putting together the first ghost-hunting kit. This was made up of essential items that he took with him on investigations. You might be surprised by some of the things he took with him to track down the things that go bump in the night—or to expose those who might be trying to pull the wool over his eyes.

Device	**Purpose**
Still and video cameras	To capture ghostly images
Phone system	To allow investigators to communicate with each other
Tape measure	To check dimensions to determine if hidden rooms are present
Pencil and paper	For taking notes and making sketches
Flashlights	To see in the dark
Mercury	Price would watch to see if ripples formed in a small bowl of mercury, indicating movement in the area (ghostly or otherwise)
Mechanical bell system	Used as a makeshift burglar alarm to alert investigators if someone (or something) had entered an area

Powder or flour	To scatter on a floor to see if anything entered the room, since it would leave footprints behind
String or twine	To set up booby traps in doorways to make sure no one entered the room
Tape	To seal off windows and doors
Powdered graphite	For developing fingerprints to determine if an activity was ghostly or not (i.e., if a person—instead of a ghost—was responsible for moving a lamp)
Felt shoe covers	To enable investigators to move around without making noise

Spending Life—and Death—Behind Bars

Life is difficult for those who are in jail. But not even death could grant the following lost souls relief from spending eternity in prison.

Andersonville Prison (Andersonville, Georgia)

Known to Confederate soldiers as "Camp Sumter," this remote prison was built during the Civil War to house captured Union soldiers. Henry Wirz, who served as captain of the site, established what he called the "Dead Line."

Anyone who crossed that line was gunned down. As was the case in most prison camps, sickness overtook many of the men. Today, visitors can still hear gunshots and sense the devastation that those prisoners must have felt long ago. A foul odor is often detected, and many people have observed ghosts walking across the grounds.

New Mexico State Penitentiary (Santa Fe, New Mexico)

A riot at the New Mexico State Penitentiary in 1980 resulted in more than enough trauma to create unsettled spirits. In a rebellion that was driven by rage rather than well-thought-out plans, 33 inmates lost their lives. Twelve guards were taken hostage, and more than 100 people were injured.

If heightened energy and emotions are the ingredients for paranormal activity, then the New Mexico State Pen should be one of the most haunted prisons in the world. And perhaps it is. Doors have been observed opening and closing on their own, lights turn on and off by themselves, unusual noises are heard, and visitors report a general feeling of unease when entering Cellblocks 3 and 4, where the worst fighting of the riots occurred. The prison was shut down in 1998 because of its "uncontrollable disturbances." It has since been used in films such as *The Longest Yard* (2005).

Cornwall Jail (Cornwall, Ontario)

One of the oldest buildings in Ontario, this jail was built in 1833. It operated as a prison until 2002. Today, the jail is a tourist attraction that allows visitors to see what prison life was like in another era. If they're lucky, visitors may also glimpse a ghost or two.

Nowadays, the prison system separates criminals by several factors, such as age, gender, and severity of crime. But that was not the case at the Cornwall Jail. In the 1800s, inmates there included both criminals and the criminally insane. Men, women, adults, and minors were all housed under one roof. Living conditions were poor, which resulted in many deaths over the years. When renovations took place in recent years, at least ten unmarked graves were found. Nearly a dozen executions by hanging and two suicides also took place on the grounds. Tourists who visit the site have heard disembodied humming and other strange noises. Doors that are locked at night are open in the morning. And some visitors report feeling the presence of a young woman and her child.

Wyoming Frontier Prison (Rawlins, Wyoming)

Known as "The Old Pen," the Wyoming Frontier Prison was built in 1901 and was used until 1981. Today, the building is a museum. The guards at the Old Pen were known for torturing the inmates. Fourteen prisoners were executed on the premises. Several more died during a botched escape attempt when death-row inmates hit a gas line while trying to tunnel their way to freedom. Someone lit a match to see what happened and the men died instantly.

But they may have been the lucky ones. Nine other death-row inmates were victims of a poorly constructed gallows. The contraption didn't drop the men far enough to break their necks, so they ended up dying slow, agonizing deaths by strangulation.

The Old Pen is now the site of several residual hauntings that feed off the negative energy of the place. Residual hauntings often create an atmosphere of unpleasantness, as if the agony that occurred there still lingers. People have reported unusual odors, screams, wailing, and a sense of intense fear. Because these are mostly residual hauntings, the spirits at the Old Pen don't seem to acknowledge the living at all, which is probably a good thing for visitors.

Testimony from the Other Side

When Zona Heaster Shue of Greenbrier County, West Virginia, died suddenly at age 23, her doctor said she died of natural causes. But when Zona's mother encountered her ghost, a shocking tale of murder was revealed. Would testimony from the Other Side help to nab Zona's killer?

Gone Too Soon

On January 23, 1897, a boy who was doing chores at the Shue home discovered Zona's body lying at the bottom of the stairs. He ran to tell her husband, Edward, and then he went to get a doctor. When Dr. George W. Knapp arrived, Edward took him to the bedroom where he'd moved Zona's lifeless body. Although Edward had already dressed Zona for burial, Dr. Knapp examined her body. As the doctor went about his duties, Edward became noticeably distressed. As a result, Dr. Knapp cut the examination short. Because he didn't want to upset Edward any further, Dr. Knapp reported Zona's cause of death as "everlasting faint." He later changed the finding to "childbirth," even though Zona hadn't told anyone that she was pregnant. During his hasty examination, Dr. Knapp noticed a few bruises on Zona's neck but quickly passed them off as unrelated.

Whirlwind Courtship

Not much is known about her life, but it is believed that Zona Heaster was born in Greenbrier County, West Virginia, around 1873. In October 1896, she met Edward Shue, a drifter who had recently moved to the area to work as a blacksmith.

Only months after they met, Zona Heaster and Edward Shue married. But for reasons that she couldn't quite explain, Zona's mother, Mary Jane Heaster, had taken an instant disliking to her son-in-law. Despite her concerns, the newlyweds seemed to get along until that tragic day when Zona was found dead. In an instant, Mary Jane's world was turned upside down. She grieved, as would any mother who must bury a child, but she strongly disagreed with

Dr. Knapp's determination of her daughter's cause of death. In her mind, there was only one way that her daughter could have died at such a young age. She believed Edward Shue had killed Zona and had covered it up.

It All Comes Out in the Wash

At Zona's funeral, those who came to pay their respects noticed Edward's strange behavior. He openly mourned his wife's passing, but something seemed odd about the way he grieved. His mood switched between extreme sadness and sudden wild energy. He tended to his wife's body like a man possessed, allowing no one to get near it. He also tied a large scarf around his wife's neck for no apparent reason. And even stranger, he placed a pillow on one side of Zona's head and a rolled-up cloth on the other. He told puzzled onlookers that they would help her "rest easier." When Zona's body was moved to the cemetery for burial, several people noticed a strange looseness to her neck as they transported her. Not surprisingly, people began to talk.

Mary Jane Heaster did not have to be convinced that Edward was acting suspiciously about Zona's death. She had always hated him and wished that her daughter had never married him. She had a sneaking suspicion that something wasn't right, but she didn't know how to prove it.

After the funeral, Mary Jane Heaster washed the sheet that had lined her daughter's coffin. To her horror, the water inside the basin turned red. Then, even more shockingly, the sheet turned pink and the water again turned clear. Convinced that this was a sign, Mary Jane began to pray that her daughter would come to her to reveal the truth. A few weeks later, her prayers were answered.

Ghostly Visions

According to Mary Jane, Zona's apparition came to her over the course of four nights. Zona described how abusive Edward had been throughout their marriage. She also stated that he was responsible for her death. The tragedy occurred because Edward thought that Zona hadn't cooked meat for supper. This sent him into a rage, and he strangled her and broke her neck. To demonstrate the brutality of Edward's attack, Zona's ghost rotated her head completely around. This horrified Mary Jane, but it also brought her some relief. Her beloved daughter had returned from the grave to seek the justice that she deserved. Armed with the power of a mother's love, Mary Jane was determined to avenge her daughter's death.

Please Believe Me!

Mary Jane immediately told local prosecutor John Alfred Preston of her ghostly visit and begged him to investigate. It is unclear whether or not he believed her story, but he agreed to interview Dr. Knapp and others connected to the case.

When John Preston found out that Dr. Knapp's examination had been rushed and less than complete, he decided that an autopsy was needed to help clear things up. It was announced that Zona's body would be dug up. A local newspaper reported that Edward Shue "vigorously complained" about this but was forced to witness the proceedings. When Dr. Knapp proclaimed that Zona's neck was indeed broken, Edward was arrested and charged with his wife's murder.

While Edward awaited trial, tales of his wicked past started coming to light. It was revealed that he'd been married twice before. His first marriage (to Allie Estelline Cutlip) had ended in divorce in 1889, while Edward was in jail for horse theft. In their divorce papers, Allie Cutlip claimed that Edward had frequently beaten her. In 1894, Edward married Lucy Ann Tritt, but the union was short-lived. Lucy died just eight months into their marriage under "mysterious" circumstances. In the autumn of 1896, Edward moved to Greenbrier County, where he met Zona Heaster. Was there a pattern of violence with this lethal ladies' man?

Trial

Edward Shue's trial began on June 22, 1897. Both the defense and the prosecution did their best to discredit each other. For every witness who spoke of Edward's ill temper, another likened him to an altar boy. Edward was poised and charismatic on the stand. Then it was Mary Jane Heaster's turn. When she was questioned by the prosecution, her ghostly encounter with her daughter was not mentioned. But when she was cross-examined by Edward's attorney, Mary Jane recalled in great detail how Zona's spirit had named Edward as her abuser and killer. The defense characterized Mary Jane's "visions" as little more than a grieving mother's ravings. They assumed that the jury would agree, but they were wrong. The jury quickly found Edward Shue guilty. Not only had they believed Mary Jane's supernatural tale, they fell just short of delivering the necessary votes to hang Edward Shue for his evil deeds. Instead, he was sentenced to life in prison. And as it turned out, that wouldn't be very long.

Conclusion

In July 1897, Edward Shue was transferred to the West Virginia Penitentiary in Moundsville, where he lived out the rest of his days. The convicted murderer died on March 13, 1900, of a disease that was spreading throughout the prison. But his name lives on, as does the ghostly legend of Zona Heaster Shue. A historical marker located beside Route 60 in Greenbrier County reads:

Greenbrier Ghost
"Interred in nearby cemetery is Zona Heaster Shue. Her death in 1897 was presumed natural until her spirit appeared to her mother to describe how she was killed by her husband Edward. Autopsy on the exhumed body verified the apparition's account. Edward, found guilty of murder, was sentenced to the state prison. Only known case in which testimony from ghost helped convict a murderer."

Spirits Shine On at the Stanley Hotel

The Stanley Hotel in Estes Park, Colorado, was the inspiration for the Overlook Hotel in Stephen King's famous novel The Shining *and the movie adaptation, which starred Jack Nicholson. Fortunately, unlike at King's fictional inn, the ghosts of the Stanley Hotel are not vengeful. But rest assured, there are definitely ghosts at this famous hotel.*

How It All Began

In 1903, Freelan Stanley—inventor of the Stanley Steamer automobile—was suffering from tuberculosis and was told that he had just months to live. So Freelan and his wife, Flora, decided to visit Estes Park hoping to find some relief in the thin mountain air. They fell in love with Estes Park's majestic Rocky Mountain landscape and decided to move there permanently.

Right away, the Stanleys started building the Stanley Hotel, which was completed in 1909. (Freelan Stanley died in 1940 at the ripe old age of 91, so apparently the mountain air did the trick.)

Nestled in the mountains, the Stanley Hotel offers a spectacular view. Many notable guests have stayed there, including American composer John Philip Sousa, President Theodore Roosevelt, Japanese royalty, members of the Hollywood elite, and, of course, writer Stephen King.

Friendly Ghosts

Stephen King stayed in Room 217, which is the haunted room in *The Shining*. But most of the paranormal activity at the Stanley seems to occur on the fourth floor, specifically in Room 418. There, guests have heard children laughing and playing, but when they complain that the kids are too loud, no children are ever found.

In Room 407, a ghost likes to play with the lights. But it's apparently a reasonable spook because when guests ask it to turn the lights back on, it does.

During his stay, Stephen King alerted the staff that a young boy on the second floor was calling for his nanny. Of course, the staff members at the Stanley were well aware of the ghostly boy, who had been spotted throughout the hotel many times over the years.

But the two most prominent spirits at the resort are those of Freelan Stanley and his wife. Flora makes her presence known by playing the piano in the ballroom. Even those who haven't seen her claim to hear piano music coming from the ballroom when it's empty. Some have even watched the piano keys move up and down by themselves.

Freelan Stanley's specter most often manifests in the lobby, the bar, and the billiard room, which were apparently his favorite spots in the hotel when he was alive.

A Ghostly Visitor

When Jason Hawes and Grant Wilson from the television show *Ghost Hunters* stayed at the Stanley Hotel in 2006, their investigation hit paranormal pay dirt. Jason stayed in Room 401, which is said to be one of the most haunted guest rooms. He set up a video camera to record anything that occurred while he was asleep. Although the picture is dark, the camera captured the distinct sounds of a door opening and glass breaking—all while Jason was sound asleep. When he got up to investigate, he noticed that the closet door had been opened and a glass on the nightstand was broken. Later, the camera recorded the closet door closing with no humans in sight.

Grant had his own paranormal experience in Room 1302. He was sitting at a table with some other team members when the table lifted off the ground and crashed back down—all by itself. When the group tried to raise the table, it was so heavy that it took several people to lift it even a few inches.

During a follow-up session at the Stanley Hotel, those in attendance were also treated to some supernatural stuff. EMF detectors were used to note changes in the electromagnetic field (which indicate that a ghost is nearby). They lit up time and again. Clear responses to questions directed at the resident spirits were also captured on audio recorders.

Meet the Spirits

The Stanley Hotel offers ghost tours to educate visitors about the paranormal activity within its walls. Or if you'd rather just stay in your room, you could always watch a movie. *The Shining* runs continuously on the guest-room televisions.

"I would not participate in [a séance] under any circumstances. Not even if my wife died and a medium said she had a message from my wife. . . . We are too close as it is to a world that is incomprehensible."

—Stephen King

"Never believe anything you hear from an inhuman haunting."

—Jason Hawes of The Atlantic Paranormal Society (TAPS)

FRIGHTENING FACTS

- *St. Mark's Church-in-the-Bowery in Manhattan was built in 1795 on the former farm of Peter Stuyvesant, who ruled New Netherland (now New York) during the 1600s. Several ghosts, notably Stuyvesant himself, make frequent appearances at St. Mark's. Stuyvesant's peg leg and cane make him easy to recognize.*

- *Before Mary Surratt was hanged for her role in Abraham Lincoln's death, she was jailed at the Federal Penitentiary, which is now Fort McNair in Washington, D.C. Perhaps the sorrowful sobs that modern residents hear are Mary's grief over her belief that she was wrongly accused.*

- *In the 1950s, the residents of 11 Bank Street in Greenwich Village often heard disembodied footsteps and unexplained pounding on the walls. One day, the homeowners found an urn containing human ashes hidden in the ceiling. After they gave the ashes a proper burial, the unexplained noises stopped.*

- *In 1959, George Reeves—television's first Superman—died of a single gunshot wound to the head at his home in Los Angeles. Ever since then, those living in his former abode have spotted a spectral Reeves (who is sometimes wearing his Superman costume) roaming the grounds. His death was ruled a suicide, but some say that his ghost has come back to tell people that he was actually murdered.*

Going on a Ghost Hunt

So you're getting ready to go on your very first ghost hunt. How exciting! But what exactly are you getting yourself into? And what's going to happen? Will you encounter shadowy shapes moving around you, hear phantom footsteps, or even see a full-bodied apparition? Read on to find out what to expect—straight from the experts.

"Do I Need to Do Anything to Prepare for the Hunt?"

Take it easy on the day of the investigation, and get a good night's sleep the day before. Also, don't eat a huge meal right before the hunt, because that might make you sleepy. And be sure to bring along some water and snacks. Being tired, hungry, or dehydrated can affect your senses, which could make you see, feel, or hear things that don't really exist. In general, just try to be as relaxed as possible.

"What's the First Thing I Should Do When I Get There?"

Get acquainted with your surroundings. Some ghost hunters like to spend a few minutes sitting quietly and absorbing as many of the sights, sounds, and even smells of the location as possible. Later, this will help you determine whether or not what you're experiencing is of a ghostly nature.

Also, because you'll probably be spending a lot of time in the dark, it helps to know your way around the location. That way, you won't be so concerned with fumbling through the darkness that you accidentally miss any paranormal activity.

"What Sort of Things Will I Do During a Ghost Hunt?"

Unlike ghost hunts on television shows, which cram entire investigations into 30- or 60-minute episodes, a full ghost hunt lasts several hours. Be prepared to spend a lot of time sitting around in the dark waiting for something to happen.

Some paranormal investigation groups like to separate the participants into smaller groups and assign them to specific areas of the haunted site. After about an hour, the groups rotate so that everyone gets some time in each area.

While at a location, you may be asked to take photos and note any temperature changes or spikes in electromagnetic field readings, which may indicate paranormal activity. You might also take part in EVP (electronic voice phenomenon) sessions. During these, you can ask questions to any spirits present. Hopefully, you'll get an otherworldly response.

Even if you don't have access to some of the super-cool ghost-hunting gear that's available now, you can always rely on your senses to "feel" the room and see if you notice anything out of the ordinary.

"What Can I Expect to See?"

If you're lucky, you just might see a ghost! But once again, it's important to get used to your surroundings. You're most likely going to be spending a lot of time in the dark, so make sure that your eyes adjust to the lack of light. "Shadow people" are moving shadows that are seen out of the corner of the eye. They are among the most commonly spotted paranormal phenomena. If you see a shadow person, take a look around to make sure that what you saw was not caused by something playing tricks on your eyes. For example, nearby streetlights can often cause tree branches blowing in the wind to cast odd shadows.

If you get really lucky, you might see what many consider the ultimate thrill in the ghost-hunting world: a full-bodied apparition. If this happens, try to remain calm and observe as much as possible, like the ghost's attire, its actions, and whether or not it seems to know that you're there. This information might help you to determine who the ghost was in life and, more importantly, why it's still hanging around.

"Will I Hear Ghosts Talking and All Sorts of Weird Noises?"

Yes, you'll probably hear lots of weird noises. Every site has its own unique set of normal noises, for example, houses settling or animals wandering through. But because the location is new to you, everything is going to sound a bit spooky. It will be up to you to decide which noises are normal and which might be *para*normal in nature. If you hear a strange noise during

an investigation, call out, "If that was you, could you please make that noise again?" If the noise repeats, it will help you figure out where it came from. It will also allow you to determine if there is a natural reason for it.

Of course, you are likely to hear voices at some point in the evening. Even if you know where all of the other ghost hunters are, remember that sounds can carry quite far, especially if you're in an empty building. If you hear a "disembodied voice," write down what it said and how it sounded. You could even ask it to repeat itself or talk louder.

"What Will I Learn?"

First and foremost, you'll learn that ghost-hunting TV shows tend to overdramatize situations. You probably won't come across any ghosts that pick you up and toss you around the room. Instead, you'll probably spend most of the investigation sitting quietly in the dark, waiting for something to happen. And if and when something *does* occur, it will happen so fast that you might not even notice it until you go back and watch your video and audio recordings from the hunt.

Most of all, you'll learn that ghost hunts are unique opportunities to explore the Other Side. After all, we all want to unravel the age-old mystery of what happens to us after we die. Have fun!

Harry Houdini: Magician and Ghost Buster

He will forever be remembered as a magician, but Harry Houdini was also a passionate ghost hunter.

Harry Houdini was skilled at magic, card tricks, and escape artistry. In fact, he set out to prove that there was nothing from which he couldn't escape. Several of Houdini's stunts were literally death defying. Once he came frighteningly close to suffocating while escaping from a buried coffin.

Another one of Houdini's well-known tricks was to swallow several needles and a piece of string. Then he would pull the string from his throat with the needles threaded. He even made a live elephant disappear at a show in New York City.

But when his mother died in 1913, Houdini was so devastated that he started going to psychics to try to contact her spirit. He soon realized that many of the mediums he visited were using the same types of tricks that magicians use. As a result, Houdini set out to expose those who were trying to deceive the public. He wore a disguise so that the psychics wouldn't recognize him. He also developed a device that kept mediums from moving, so they couldn't fake supernatural activity after the lights were turned off.

Don't Stop Believing . . .

Even though Houdini knew that some mediums were conning the public, he never stopped believing that life continued after death. He even promised his wife that if he could reach out to her after he died, he would. They created a secret code that only the two of them knew, so that if his wife was given a message from a psychic, she would know whether or not it was really from him. After Houdini died on October 31, 1926, his wife held numerous séances at their home in New York City. But she was never able to make contact with her husband's spirit. However, several people who later lived in Houdini's home claimed that they saw the ghost of the world-famous magician.

The Last Run of the *Montreal Express*

Restless spirits wander around the site of a major train wreck. Are they searching for answers, hoping to be rescued, or trying to prevent the disaster? Perhaps it's all of the above.

Sites of tragedies are hot spots for paranormal activity. In fact, such sites seem to feature all of the critical elements that are known to attract ghosts. First and foremost, they have the "taken away too soon" factor. Haven't we all heard about souls that remain earthbound simply because their mortal stays were cut short? Tragedy sites also feature a distinct "if only I could have warned them" element. Spirits with this mindset feel that they could have prevented a particular tragedy if only they'd done this or that. Finally, there's the "why did you leave me?" aspect. This is the very sad question that ghosts and survivors alike ask when loved ones suddenly and unexpectedly die. The case of 13-year-old Joe McCabe falls into this category. But others who lost their lives during the doomed run of the *Montreal Express* on February 5, 1877, span all of the above.

Vermont's Worst Train Wreck

One moment, the *Montreal Express* was chugging through the night, passing over a wooden bridge at White River Junction, Vermont. The next minute, it was lying in a heap on solid river ice more than 40 feet below. During the crash, gas lamps were knocked over and burst into flames. But the situation got even worse when the huge wooden bridge above the train caught on fire. Many people tried to help, but the intense heat and smoke prevented them from doing so. They could only listen to the anguished cries of the unfortunate souls who were trapped in the wreckage. The horrors were unimaginable. Some victims were burned to death; others were crushed. And, in a cruel twist of fate, some slowly drowned as the fiery cars melted through the ice. Despite the valiant efforts of rescuers, 34 people died.

It was later discovered that the train had passed over a damaged piece of railway, which caused four of its cars to jump the tracks. This hardly consoled the survivors and grieving families. Their lives had been changed forever the instant that the train left the tracks. The bridge was eventually rebuilt—this time out of steel—and life went on as always. But the crash site wasn't quite ready to let go of its tragic past.

Ghosts in Training

The Paine House is located beside the bridge where the crash occurred. After the accident, it was used as a temporary hospital. It is one of the few structures there that remains from the time of the crash, and the supernatural energy in the house is off the charts! The kitchen ceiling is stained red from the blood of the crash victims. (It seeped through the floorboards from the room above, where the injured and dead were placed.) Mysterious noises and loud sobbing have been heard coming from the empty house. And there are stories that animals were too frightened to enter the barn.

At the crash site, many people have seen a man dressed in a railway uniform patrolling the empty tracks at night. Some believe that it's the ghost of the train's conductor, Mr. Sturtevant. As the doomed *Montreal Express* made its way onto the wooden bridge, Sturtevant felt an unfamiliar grinding. Sensing trouble, he instinctively yanked the bell cord to warn the engineer to stop, but it was too late. Even with its brakes fully applied, the train jumped the tracks and tumbled into the icy river below.

Perhaps the saddest tale from this incident involves young Joe McCabe. Just 13 years old at the time of the tragedy, the boy survived the wreck only to suffer the pain of watching his father burn to death. Today, the ghostly boy can sometimes be seen hovering just above the river, praying that his father will somehow survive. But it's useless. Joe McCabe's greatest wish will never come true. It appears that he's destined to replay the most tragic event of his life over and over again.

Don't Mess with the Lady in Black

At the start of the Civil War, Andrew Lanier was preparing to leave his home in Georgia to serve in the Confederate Army. But before he left, he asked his beloved girlfriend Melanie to marry him. She did, and the two spent just one night together as husband and wife. The next day, Andrew headed off to war, probably thinking that he would return home soon. Little did he or Melanie know that they would never again see each other as a free man and woman.

A few months later, Andrew was captured by Union forces. He was sent to Fort Warren, a military prison on Georges Island, which is located about seven miles off the coast of Boston. As military prisons go, Fort Warren was not as bad as some others. But to Andrew it was unbearable. He deeply missed Melanie, and he told her so in a letter.

After Melanie read the letter, she knew that she could not stand by and do nothing while her husband rotted away in prison. So she cut her hair short, disguised herself as a man, and made her way across Union lines to Massachusetts. Finally, during a violent storm, she managed to slip inside the prison, which was not terribly secure. (Remember, Fort Warren was on an island. It was thought that even if a prisoner escaped from Fort Warren, he would have nowhere to go since he was in the frigid Atlantic Ocean, seven miles from land.) Soon, Melanie was reunited with her husband.

Foiled and Spoiled

The fort's other prisoners were probably happy to see a Southern woman in their midst. They were certainly glad that she had brought along an old pistol and a short-handled pick. The prisoners hatched a scheme to tunnel underneath the fort's arsenal, where the weapons were stored. Once there, they planned to grab guns and seize the fort. Then they would turn their guns on Boston.

The prisoners worked on the tunnel for the next few weeks. However, they had miscalculated the distance to the arsenal. When they tried to break through the ground, they were caught. One by one, they came out of the tunnel—except for Melanie. She had planned to wait until all of the others had exited the tunnel. Then she was going to pop out of the hole with her pistol and take the guards by surprise.

It was a long shot, but it might have worked. Unfortunately, after Melanie came out of the hole and ordered the guards to surrender, they quickly formed a circle around her and closed in. Just as Melanie pulled the trigger on her gun, it was knocked from her hand. The wayward bullet struck her husband and killed him instantly. Melanie was captured and was sentenced to hang as a Confederate spy.

On the day of her execution, Melanie made a final request. She wanted to wear a dress for the hanging instead of the men's clothing that she had been wearing for weeks. She was given an old black dress. That should have been the end… but it was only the beginning.

Un-"fort"-unate Occurrences

A short time later, a soldier named Cassidy was patrolling the area near where Melanie had died. Suddenly, he felt two hands grab him around the neck from behind. The hands tried to strangle him. Struggling for breath, Cassidy managed

to twist around so that he could see his attacker. He was staring into the ghostly face of Melanie Lanier.

Wearing the black dress in which she had died, Melanie stared at the soldier. Her face was pale, but her eyes were full of hatred and revenge. Cassidy screamed, and managed to wriggle out of her grip. He ran back to the other guards, crying out in terror. But the other guards laughed at his story, and Cassidy was locked away in the guardhouse for 30 days for deserting his post. That was just fine with him because he vowed never to patrol that area after dark again.

The "Lady in Black" has been haunting Fort Warren ever since then. In 1891, female footprints were found in the snow, even though no woman had been on the island. Then, during World War II, an army lookout encountered the ghost of Melanie Lanier near the site where she died. He was so frightened by the incident that he went insane and spent the next two decades in a mental institution.

A few years after World War II, Captain Charles Norris was stationed alone on the island. He was reading one night when he felt someone tap him on the shoulder. He turned around, but no one was there.

Later, when the telephone began to ring, Captain Norris answered it only to hear the operator ask, "What number please?" Norris explained that he was answering a call, not making one. The operator said that Norris's wife had answered the phone previously and had taken a message. But Norris was all alone on the island. He knew that only one female could have answered the phone: the Lady in Black.

Melanie's vengeful spirit still roams Fort Warren. Guards on duty there have been known to shoot at misty forms, and once, a stone rolled all the way across a floor under its own power. It seems that Melanie is still trying to find ways to distract the guards stationed there. After all, it was her love for her husband that brought her to the island, and even though they're both long dead, her love—like her spirit—lives on.

RIP RIP RIP RIP

"Moore" Ghosts Gather in Villisca

Villisca, Iowa, was once a bustling town. In the early 1900s, it was home to more than 2,500 citizens, a busy train station, and dozens of businesses. But on June 10, 1912, a local family was brutally murdered in their home. The crime was never solved, and the town has since dwindled in size to about half as many residents. You might say that Villisca has become a ghost town . . . literally.

How It All Began—and Ended

On the evening of June 9, 1912, Josiah Moore, his wife Sarah, and their four children attended a church event. Afterward, the Moores, as well as Lena and Ina

Stillinger—two young neighbor girls who were sleeping over—returned home and went to bed.

The next morning, Mary Peckham, the Moores' next-door neighbor, went outside to hang her laundry. She was surprised by the silence that greeted her from the Moore house. After all, a family of six was rarely quiet. Mary called Josiah's brother Ross, who came over to check things out.

Bungled Bungalow

Ross unlocked the door and entered the parlor. The home was covered in a blanket of eerie silence. But when he opened the door to one of the bedrooms, he was confronted with a horrific sight: the bloody bodies of the Stillinger girls lying in a bed.

Mary Peckham called the police. When the police arrived, they found the lifeless bodies of Josiah, Sarah, Herman, Katherine, Boyd, and Paul Moore, as well as the Stillinger girls. They had all been brutally murdered with an ax. The murder weapon had been wiped off and left by the door.

That the crime was never solved is no real surprise due to the mayhem that followed. As word of the murders spread, friends and hundreds of curious onlookers raced to the house. The police soon lost control of the crime scene. With all of this chaos and none of today's technology, the police were unable to solve the case. This haunted them for the rest of their lives.

The Suspects

Among the leading suspects was Frank F. Jones, a local businessman. He was angry with Josiah for leaving his company and taking one of its best clients. People who believe that Jones was behind the murders think that he hired hit man William Mansfield to do the dirty work. Although police were suspicious of the pair, they did not find enough evidence to prosecute either of them.

Another school of thought suggests that a drifter committed the murders. Two men fit that description. Andy Sawyer was a vagrant who traveled with an ax. Henry Moore (no relation to the victims) was later convicted of killing his mother and grandmother with an ax and was a suspect in several other ax murders. But there was no evidence to connect either man to the Villisca crimes.

Traveling preacher George Kelly was another prime suspect. He had been present at the church event that the Moores attended right before they were killed. George also left town the morning that the bodies were discovered. He reportedly told passengers on the train that he'd had a vision that told him to "Slay and slay utterly." When he was arrested for another crime in 1914, he admitted to the Moore murders but later withdrew his confession. Nevertheless, George

Kelly was tried twice for the Moore murders. One trial ended in a hung jury, and he was acquitted in the other.

If You Renovate It, They Will Come

After the murders, the Moore house changed hands several times because, really, who wants to live in a house where eight people were killed? By 1994, the house was in danger of being torn down. That's when a realtor came up with an idea. Darwin and Martha Linn owned the Olson-Linn Museum in Villisca. The realtor asked them if they'd be interested in purchasing the Moore house to preserve another piece of the town's history. They were.

Using old photographs, the Linns restored the house to its 1912 condition and decorated it with items from back then. They even removed the electricity, water, and bathrooms.

After the renovation was complete, the Linns began giving tours of the house. On these tours, visitors get a glimpse of Villisca in the early 1900s. They also learn the details of the gruesome murders, including possible suspects and how the crime and the trial of Reverend Kelly affected the small town.

They're Baaaaack

With the house looking almost exactly as it had in 1912, it seems that the spirits of the Moore family were drawn back to it. Visitors have reported seeing ghosts and hearing young girls crying. Closet doors open and close by themselves, and balls mysteriously roll across the floor.

Darwin Linn said that he'd heard stories about the spirits at the Moore house. But he didn't believe them . . . until he saw the kids who came through the house on tours. He saw them interacting with other children—children who weren't there. "That makes the hair stand up on the back of my head," he said. Now, he's convinced that the Moore family is still around.

Many ghost hunters have toured the house and found proof of spirits there. Ghostly blobs have been captured in photos. Mysterious voices have been recorded on audio devices. Maritza Skandunas, the founder of San Diego Ghost Hunters, collected some of the spookiest evidence. She told her scary tale on the TV show *My Ghost Story*.

1912 Again

Maritza decided that she wanted to spend the night in the creepy old house. "It felt like you went back a hundred years," she said. "You could almost relive what they felt and the screaming that must have been going on . . . ."

As Maritza and her friends walked through the house absorbing its evil energy, they were able to imagine what took place in each room. Soon, they noticed a black shadow following them. They believe that it was the spirit of the murderer. Maritza said that it gave off "a very hateful energy."

In the master bedroom, Maritza felt something touch her arm. When she took a picture of the room's mirror, she saw the image of Sarah Moore staring back at her in the photo.

In one of the kids' rooms, the investigators asked Herman, the oldest of the Moore children, to open the closet door. The door opened all by itself, even though no one was near it. But soon after that, the black shadow appeared again, and Maritza and her friends began to feel sick to their stomachs. The killer obviously didn't want any happiness in the house. But when the group left the room, an audio recorder captured the voice of a child saying, "Don't go."

Evil Energy

In 2010, the team from *Ghost Adventures* visited the Villisca Ax Murder House. During their investigation, an audio recorder picked up a chilling EVP (electronic voice phenomenon) that said, "I killed six kids." That was enough to send shivers down the spines of the ghost hunters and make a believer of a skeptic they'd brought along.

"We are all spirit. When we pass on, we simply get rid of the outer layer and, underneath, there really is a duplicate layer. This inner body—like an inner tube of a tire—is where our personality resides. At death the physical body is worn out and dissolved, so the inner body is where we live."

—Hans Holzer, famous paranormal researcher

Celebrities Who've Encountered Ghosts

Celebrities are only human, so it's not surprising that many of them have had run-ins with ghosts. Here are a few terrifying tales of stars who have collided with the spirit world.

Haylie Duff

Best known for her role on the TV show *7th Heaven* and in the film *Napoleon Dynamite* (2004), actress Haylie Duff is also the older sister of singer/actress Hillary Duff. She's also a strong believer in the spirit world—and not just because she's had a personal encounter with it.

In the early 2000s, Haylie went to audition for a role in a movie. She met with the director, Joe, and the two of them immediately hit it off. They just seemed to have a strange connection—like they were old friends.

That night, Haylie woke up around 3:30 A.M. She was shocked to see a Buddhist woman standing at the foot of her bed. After a short time, the woman disappeared and Haylie was left with the feeling that Joe had died.

The next morning, Haylie received a phone call from Joe's business partner. The woman told Haylie that Joe had died of a heart attack the night before—at the exact time that Haylie had seen the Buddhist woman in her bedroom. The business partner also told Haylie that Joe was a Buddhist.

Haylie believes that the Buddhist woman was actually Joe who came to her when he died because he felt a special connection to her. She also thinks that he took the form of a woman so that she wouldn't be frightened to see a man standing in her room in the middle of the night.

Michael Urie

Michael Urie is best known for his role as Marc St. James, Betty's arch-nemesis on the TV show *Ugly Betty.* After he graduated from drama school, Michael was sharing an apartment in New York City with his friend Megan. One night, the two were hanging out with some friends at their apartment when someone suggested playing with a Ouija board. That made Megan uncomfortable, so she went to her room. Michael and his friends decided to consult the Ouija board anyway.

When the group asked, "Who's there?" the board spelled out, "Billy." When they asked Billy what he wanted, the board spelled, "Megan." This sent chills down the spines of Michael and his buddies. Michael asked Megan to come out of her room, and she immediately said, "Is it Billy?" It was then that she told them that Billy was a childhood friend of hers who had died in a car accident at age 13. She said that whenever someone uses a Ouija board in her presence, Billy always shows up. Not surprisingly, this terrified Megan. She asked Billy to leave her apartment.

Later that night, Michael woke up when Megan's dog started barking ferociously as if there was an intruder in the house. When Michael and Megan went to investigate, the dog was growling at something in the living room that they couldn't see. Michael went into the kitchen, and as he was about to go back to bed, he saw the shadowy figure of a boy who he believes was Billy.

Bret Michaels

In the early 1980s, Bret Michaels was a struggling musician living near Pittsburgh, Pennsylvania. He knew he wanted to be a rock star, but he just didn't know how to break out of his small town.

One day, Bret was hanging out in his buddy's basement when he saw a strange light in the corner of the room. His friend didn't see it. A short time later, Bret again saw a glowing orb of light floating slowly across the room. He was so scared that he ran out of the basement. Even though this terrified him, it also motivated him to move to Los Angeles and form the band Poison. That was the big break he needed to fulfill his lifelong dream of being a rock star.

Fast forward to the early 1990s. Bret was in his house in Malibu, California, when he felt someone come up from behind him and hug him. He thought it was his girlfriend, so he turned around. No one (living) was there, but he briefly saw the ghost of his beloved grandmother.

Nick Hogan

Nick Hogan is the son of wrestling legend Hulk Hogan and part of the cast of the show *Hogan Knows Best.* In 2004, Nick and some of his buddies decided to spend a night in a hotel that was rumored to be haunted. A murder had supposedly taken place on the 5th floor in the early 1900s. Since then, that floor had been sealed and nobody was allowed up there.

Being curious teenage boys, Nick and his friends decided to sneak up to the 5th floor to check things out. They figured the door to the floor would be locked. But when they got there, the door opened all by itself as if it was inviting them in.

The 5th floor was a lot different from the rest of the hotel. For one thing, it was much colder, even though there was no air conditioning and it was a hot summer night in Florida. As the boys continued to investigate, Nick shined his flashlight in each of the old guest rooms. In one particular room, he saw a shadow figure. He told his buddies about it, but they didn't believe him. But they soon would....

When the boys peered into the last room, Nick and his friends saw a dark shadow move across the room and come toward them. Then it growled at them and said, "Get back to where you came from!" The boys ran down the hall toward the stairs. But on the way, Nick stopped and looked at a mirror in one of the rooms. In it, he saw what he believes was a replay of the murder that took place there so long ago.